# JAGUAR

## XJR

## GROUP C & GTP CARS

### A TECHNICAL
### APPRAISAL OF
### THE V12 CARS

# JAGUAR

## XJR

## GROUP C & GTP CARS

### A TECHNICAL
### APPRAISAL OF
### THE V12 CARS

IAN BAMSEY

A **FOULIS** Motoring Book

First published 1989

© RACECAR ENGINEERING

Published by:
Haynes Publishing Group, Sparkford, Near Yeovil,
Somerset BA22 7JJ, England

Haynes Publications Inc., 861 Lawrence Drive, Newbury
Park, California 91320, USA

Produced for G.T. Foulis & Co. Ltd. by
**RACECAR ENGINEERING** (Specialist Publications)
6, Foundry House, Stars Lane, Yeovil, Somerset, BA20
1NL, England

Editorial Director: Ian Bamsey
Research Assistant: Alan Lis

*The colour photographs in this book have been supplied by :*
Jaguar Cars PLC and Colin Taylor Productions.
The black and white photographs are from those sources
and also John Overton, Robert and Lisa Newsome, LAT
and the Racecar Engineering Collection.

British Library Cataloguing in Publication Data

Bamsey, Ian
Jaguar XJR
1. Jaguar V12 racing cars 1985 to 1988
I. Title
629.2'28

ISBN 0-85429-752-9

Library of Congress Catalog Card number 89-80119

Printed in England by:
Wincanton Litho, Wincanton, Somerset
DTP & Artwork by:
Graphic Examples, Sherborne, Dorset

10
INTRODUCTION

## V12

14
JAGUAR V12
26
GROUP 44
40
TWR

## 1985

44
KIDLINGTON BRIEFING
54
TWR V12
58
XJR-6
64
XJR-6 RIVALS
70
XJR-6 ON TRACK

## 1986

78
KIDLINGTON BRIEFING
80
XJR-6
82
XJR-6 RIVALS
83
XJR-6 ON TRACK

## 1987

100
KIDLINGTON BRIEFING
102
XJR-8
105
XJR-8 RIVALS
106
XJR-8 ON TRACK

## 1988

126
KIDLINGTON BRIEFING
127
XJR-9
129
XJR-9 RIVALS
135
XJR-9 ON TRACK

# INTRODUCTION

As these words are written Tom Walkinshaw Racing is testing the machine that will defend its World Sports-Prototype Championship and Le Mans rule in 1989. For the first time since it commenced its Group C programme, TWR is starting the season with a brand new car. Designed to counter a growing threat from Daimler-Benz, its arrival marks the end of an era. The era of the XJR-6/8/9, one of the few racing cars ever to win a Design Council Award in addition to track success.

The Award confirms selection by the council as "an outstanding British product", and TWR's first Group C car was just that. Designed in 1985, it was developed over four seasons tasting success in 1986, consistent success in 1987 and Le Mans glory in 1988. Le Mans was the victory Jaguar wanted above all, the marque having made its reputation with a series of Le Mans victories in the Fifties.

In those far off days the factory's research and development department could enter into the business of winning motor races. But motor racing became increasingly specialised, calling for the skill of a specialist operation. To return to Le Mans in the Eighties, Jaguar put its fortunes in the hands of experts, first Group 44 then TWR. Two of the few specialist racing teams to have engine expertise.

TWR Team Owner Tom Walkinshaw had taken the decision to create his own Engine Division early on. That set TWR aside from the mass of specialist British based racing teams. To operate Engine Division Walkinshaw appointed a Kiwi engine man who had run a successful tuning 'shop back home but whose name was unknown in Britain. Walkinshaw is renowned as a talent spotter and Allan Scott would, in time, gain worldwide recognition through the success of his work for TWR.

Walkinshaw masterminded the TWR operation but did not manage it. Good management is central to the success of a team so Walkinshaw again chose his man carefully. Roger Silman had organised the Toleman team's difficult transition from customer car Formula Two team to major Grand Prix car manufacturer. On behalf of Walkinshaw, Silman developed TWR from a saloon racing operation into a team capable of fielding a Le Mans winning car.

That car was designed by Scott and chassis expert Tony Southgate. Southgate was another careful choice. He had a fine track record and his Jaguar V12 design for TWR raised the level of Group C chassis performance in spite of the packaging difficulties posed by a long, top heavy stock block engine. The XJR-6 introduced a higher level of technology and pushed forward the science-cum-black art of sports-prototype aerodynamics. It is significant that Sauber had to switch from Porsche 956-influenced aerodynamics to XJR-6-influenced aerodynamics to be able to challenge TWR with its potent Mercedes-engined turbocar.

The success of the TWR XJR-6/8/9 was all the more remarkable when one considers that Scott was tackling a fuel efficiency orientated formula with an unblown two valve stock block engine. An engine designed back in the days when Jaguar was in racing with its research and development department. The Coventry V12 was one of the oldest engines competing in the Eighties yet, thanks to the efforts of the team Walkinshaw created at Kidlington, near Oxford it was one of the most successful.

This book looks at the background to that success, tracing the Group 44 effort that paved the way for the Kidlington onslaught. It then looks in detail at the making of a Le Mans winner. The technology of the TWR V12 cars is explored on a year-by-year basis, highlighting strengths and weaknesses and chassis and engine developments. Such an investigation would not have been possible without the generous co-operation of key members of the TWR team, in particular Scott, Silman, Southgate and TWR chassis development engineer Alastair McQueen.

The author is also grateful for the equally enthusiastic assistance given by members of the opposition, in particular Daimler-Benz' engine development engineer Gert Withalm and Sauber Technical Director Leo Ress. Their help made it possible to provide a full insight into the design and development of the car that rose to challenge TWR's domination of the World Championship. A racing car can only be judged against its opposition and the book also probes the Porsche that was so hard to prise from its grip upon Le Mans. Here Porsche personnel Peter Falk, Hans Mezger and Jurgen Barth provided valuable assistance.

Le Mans was the victory Jaguar coveted above all. What it took to dislodge Porsche was a well equipped and highly effective racing team and that is what TWR provided for Jaguar. This book aims to give a full, fair and accurate appraisal of TWR's weaponry through the first, V12 era .

# The Magic World

The Jaguar V12 engine was designed to win Le Mans in 1958 rather than 1988. Jaguar, of course, first won Le Mans in 1951 with the C-type and went on to win again in 1953, then in 1955 and '56 with the charismatic D-type. However, by the late Fifties World Championship sports car racing had developed into a battle between 4.0 litre V12 Ferrari and 4.5 litre V8 Maserati runners leaving Jaguar's 3.4 litre straight six breathless. A Le Mans win by an enlarged, 3.8 litre D-type in 1957 was a classic triumph of endurance over speed. It was achieved by a factory supported but privately entered car: the works had withdrawn pending development of a 5.0 litre V12 replacement engine...

Whereas the straight six 'XK' engine had been a production engine subsequently modified for racing, the new V12 was to be first and foremost a racing engine, one capable of sustaining the marque's World Sports Car Championship competitiveness through the late Fifties. However, a large capacity V12 was perceived as the type of engine Jaguar wanted in a future production car. Work began in 1955, the design team headed by Claude Baily who, together with Walter Hassan, had been centrally involved in the design of the XK engine masterminded by Engineering Chief William Heynes.

Serious consideration had been given to the V12 configuration during the genesis of the XK engine soon after the war but six cylinders was, significantly at that time, a more practical choice. The XK engine featured a Weslake-influenced crossflow hemispherical combustion chamber with a 70 degree included valve angle. Its two valves were operated by chain driven twin overhead camshafts. The head was cast in aluminium to save weight and its general characteristics were adopted by the Baily V12. However, the valve angle was narrowed to 60 degrees for a slightly shallower chamber and downdraught inlet ports were introduced for improved breathing.

Baily based his engine on a 60 degree vee angle aluminium block fitted with iron liners of 87.0mm. bore. The crankshaft was steel and provided a 70.0mm. stroke for a total displacement of 4994.0cc. Running in seven main bearings, it was turned by steel con rods which were driven by semi-slipper type pistons. Each bank had its own chain drive from the front end while a third chain drove one pressure and two scavenge pumps for the dry sump oil system.

Performance well in excess of the XK racing engine, which was hard pressed to exceed 300b.h.p.

even in 3.8 litre guise, was anticipated. However, the potential went untested. Increasing power outputs had been worrying the powers that be: from 1958 onwards World Championship sports car races were run to a 3.0 litre capacity limit. The Baily engine (drawn by one Tom Jones) did not resurface until 1964, by which stage unlimited capacity sports-prototypes were once again welcome at Le Mans.

By the end of 1964 the V12 had been translated into metal and was running on the test bench. Lucas mechanical injection and conventional (contact breaker and coil) ignition allowed the engine to run to just over 8,000r.p.m. and with a 10.4:1 compression ratio and running Shell 100 octane power was later quoted as "502b.h.p. at 7,600r.p.m." with torque of "386lb.ft. at 6,300r.p.m." On the face of it, given the lack of development, that was encouraging: the 1964 4.0 litre Ferrari V12 produced around 370b.h.p. The 100b.h.p. per litre Jaguar engine was planned to propel a new mid engine sports-prototype chassis produced in house but early in 1965 Jaguar had a sudden change of heart and cancelled the project.

Ford was now making a very heavily funded bid for Le Mans honours and Jaguar was running into financial difficulties: in 1966 it merged with BMC. That and the imposition in mid '67 of another 3.0 litre sports-prototype capacity limit sealed the fate of the racing V12. However, a wet sump version of the Baily engine was taken as the starting point for a new V12 production power plant.

The production V12 was designed by a team again directed by Heynes - still Jaguar's Engineering Chief - and including Baily, Hassan and Harry Mundy. Hassan had spent time working at Coventry Climax on its early Sixties Grand Prix engines, while Mundy was another ex-Climax man. Early in '63 Jaguar had bought Coventry Climax Engines Ltd. Hassan had stayed at Climax to the end of the 1.5 litre Grand Prix engine programme then, in '66, had moved back to Jaguar's Browns Lane plant where he persuaded Mundy to join him. Sadly, Baily had a stroke which put him out of action for a while, then in 1969 Heynes retired and was replaced by Hassan. Hassan stayed on until 1972, just long enough to see the revamped V12 launched in a 'Series III' E-type.

Hassan later admitted he had been unimpressed by the twin cam Baily engine as a racing power plant. In his autobiography 'Climax in Coventry' (MRP 1975) he noted that its 100b.h.p. per litre was disappointing when "over at Coventry Climax we were accustomed to seeing more than 130b.h.p. per litre on Grand Prix designs. Even if one had conceded a little power to aid endurance running, say to 120b.h.p. per litre, this should have resulted in a 5.0 litre Jaguar producing around 600b.h.p., considerably more than was ever achieved by this four cam engine. There were, in addition, other puzzles. Not only was there a lack of top end power, there was also a distinct lack of low speed and mid range torque".

However, Hassan points out that by the time he became involved, the Jaguar V12's raison d'etre had changed from racing to road application. In this respect, Jaguar was the first British manufacturer since the war to produce a V12 engine. Through the Fifties and Sixties the configuration had become the hallmark of Ferrari: even Rolls-Royce found eight cylinders sufficient. Jaguar saw an obvious appeal for a V12 in America, where eight cylinders was commonplace among home grown performance cars. It claimed it was bringing "the magic world of twelve cylinder motoring to a far wider selection of automobile connoisseurs than ever before".

On a practical level, a V12 runs as two six cylinder engines sharing a common crankshaft and with a 60 degree vee angle retains the characteristic smoothness of the straight six. Hassan and Mundy pointed to the perfect balance of the 60 degree V12 for smooth running but surprised enthusiasts by abandoning the classic Jaguar hemispherical twin cam head. This was primarily to keep the more complex unit as light, compact and quiet as possible.

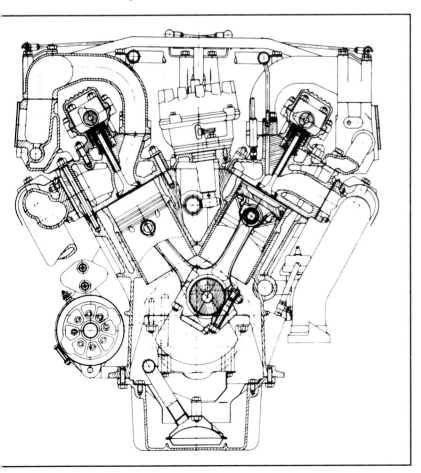

With single cam heads the V12 was able to squeeze into the same underbonnet space as the XK engine, and was cheaper to produce. It was not required to run beyond 6,500r.p.m. and the chosen single cam head provided vertical in line valves adequate for breathing up to that level. The combustion chamber was of another Weslake-pioneered design: the head was flat with the chamber formed entirely as a depression in the piston crown. Fairly deep bowl-in-piston chambers were evaluated but better performance was extracted from a shallower, wider chamber in spite of the reduced squish area (which avoided the need for valve clearance notches). It was established that with this design the sparking plug was best located near the centre, firing from the inlet side.

Further tests showed that the s.o.h.c. flathead design was better in all respects than the d.o.h.c. hemi-head up to 5,000r.p.m. Bench tests revealed a stronger torque curve and less exhaust emission and these were followed by conclusive road tests, a Mk10 saloon equipped with the new engine running alongside a similar model running the wet sump derivative of the racing engine. A full account of the birth of the engine was given by Mundy in an Institute of Mechanical Engineers paper of October 1971.

With an eye to the American market exhaust emission was of great concern and this was the reason for a switch from Lucas mechanical injection to carburettors and for a lowering of the compression ratio from 10.6 to 9.0:1, allowing the use of 97 octane fuel. A pair of Stromberg 175 CD SE carburettors fed each bank of the engine and although the semi-downdraught inlet ports were designed to be fed from within the vee the inlet tracts swept over the respective camshaft to allow the carburettors to be located outside, above the exhaust manifolding. Locating the carburettors outside kept the overall height down for a lower bonnet line and the long sweeping tracts were claimed to produce a mid-range torque improving ram effect.

Ignition, for the first time on a production car, was by the transistorised Lucas 'Opus' system. Developed from Grand Prix racing, the MkII Opus system was able to deliver 700 sparks per second at 6,000r.p.m., comfortably in excess of the V12 engine's 600 per second requirement at that speed. Earlier transistor-assisted systems had retained the points as a trigger carrying low current, with the switching of coil current taken care of by a power transistor. However, in view of the low current needed to trigger the transistor it had been possible to switch the mechanical contact breaker for an electro-magnetic pick up on the crankshaft, and this was the innovation of the Opus system which ensured consistent timing through the engine's working life.

The chosen capacity was 5343.0cc from an over-square 90.0 x 70.0mm., a stroke:bore ratio of 0.779:1. While a fuel injected version had given over 300b.h.p., the 'clean' production engine was quoted as producing 272 b.h.p./5,850 r.p.m. with maximum torque of 304 lb.ft. at 3,600 r.p.m. Impressively, torque was in excess of 240 lb.ft. right the way from 1,100 to 5,800 r.p.m.

A major departure from the XK series was an alloy block, as per the Baily racing engine. Indeed, the block, heads, sump, oil cooler, timing covers, coolant pump casing, tappet block, cam covers and induction manifolds were all light alloy castings to help save weight. In spite of the engine's displacement, it weighed little more than Jaguar's biggest, 4.2 litre six cylinder iron engine. Jaguar claimed its light alloy construction saved 116lb. over a comparable iron engine.

The sand-cast LM25 aluminium alloy block extended from open-top decks to a depth of four inches below the crankshaft axis. The crankshaft was retained by four-bolt cast iron caps. This ensured adequate rigidity for the avoidance of crankshaft rumble and reduced to a minimum variations in clearance due to thermal expansion. The block carried cast iron liners retained by a flange resting on a shelf located 44.4mm. from the top of the bore. This ensured the hottest upper portion of the liner was in direct contact with the coolant while minimising problems due to differential expansion of the iron liner and alloy block. Holymar sealing compound was used to prevent any possibility of leakage at the flange while Cooper ring seals were employed between the liner and the sand-cast alloy head, which was retained by 26 bolts.

Each head carried a die-cast alloy tappet block with seven integral camshaft bearings closed by die-cast alloy caps. The cast iron camshaft operated the in-line vertical valves directly through cast iron bucket tappets with shim-adjustment. The valves ran in cast iron guides and the head was fitted with 90 degree iron valve seats. Each valve was closed by a single spring. The inlet valve was EN 52 silicon chrome steel, the exhaust 21-4NS austenitic steel, both having a diameter of 7.74mm. Lift was inlet 41.8mm, exhaust 34.6mm. and valve crash speed was quoted as 7,840 r.p.m.

The shallow-chamber indented, fully skirted pistons were die cast light alloy carrying three plain rings, two compression one oil control. The con rod was attached via a conventional, circlip retained gudgeon pin. The forged steel rod was of typical I-section with a bronze-bushed small end and had a two-bolt big end cap. Both big end and main bearings were supplied by Vandervell and were of the usual steel-backed copper-lead thinwall type.

The three-plane, seven bearing crankshaft was a EN 16T manganese molybdenum steel forging with 3.0 inch diameter main bearing, 2.3 inch diameter big end journals. The crankshaft was Tuftrided and was balanced statically and dynamically and was equipped with a rubber/ steel vibration damper in view of its harmonic characteristics. As with the racing engine, the camshaft drive was taken off the front end via a

COLOUR PAGES 17 - 24:

# V12 On Track

*The Jaguar V12 engine commenced its professional racing career in the mid Seventies: Broadspeed in England tackled the European Touring Car Championship with a XJ12 coupe while Group 44 in the USA entered an XJ-S in the Trans Am Championship. While the Broadspeed adventure quickly fizzled out in disgrace, Bob Tullius' American campaign brought considerable success. That success led to a Trans Am-engined sports-prototype, the Group 44 XJR-5 which was built to contest IMSA's GTP category.*

*The XJR-5 was designed to have long term Le Mans potential and after a full season of IMSA competition in 1983 Group 44 took the name of Jaguar back to the classic 24 hour race. Tullius' smartly prepared GTP cars ran at La Sarthe in 1984 and 1985 (pages 18-19) but did not find competitive pace against the rival Group C machines. The Le Mans effort lacked vital Group C experience and in 1985 Jaguar backed a second sports-prototype team, Tom Walkinshaw Racing, this one based in England and involved in Group C fulltime.*

*The TWR Group C XJR-6 had its own racing version of the V12 (page 17) and the car arrived to contest the latter half of the 1985 World Championship, making its home debut at Brands Hatch (pages 20-21). The British Racing Green machine gave way to a Silk Cut liveried challenger in 1986 and in 1987 XJR-6 was replaced by the modified XJR-8 (pages 22-23), the model which dominated the 1987 World Championship. However, the special version built for Le Mans (page 24) did not claim the most coveted prize of all. That was taken by the 1988 XJR-9, a cutaway drawing of which appears in black and white on pages 8-9.*

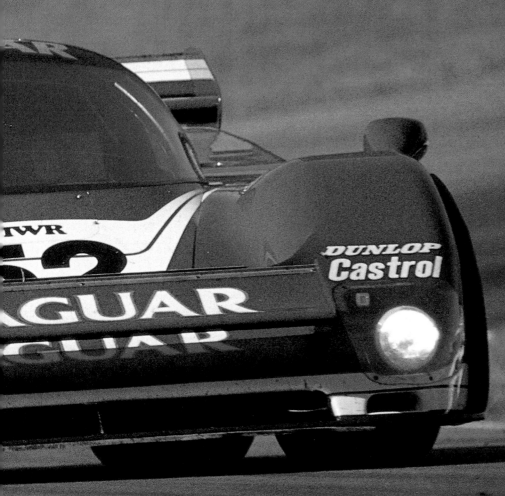

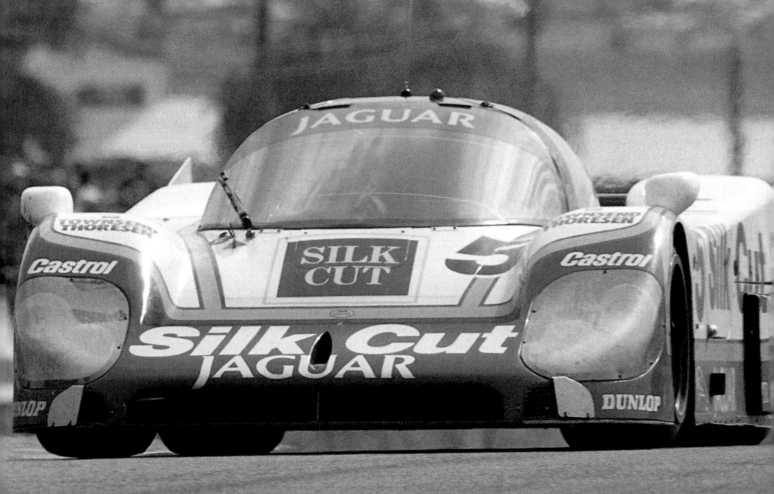

chain, but in view of the single camshaft per bank had been simplified somewhat. Only one Duplex chain was employed, driven by a 21 tooth sprocket located ahead of the front main bearing. The 9.5mm. pitch two-row chain was tensioned by a new type of tensioner developed by the Morse Chain Division of Borg-Warner.

In addition to the camshaft the chain drove a jackshaft running down the centre of the vee and of the four runs of chain between the four sprockets, three were controlled by damper pads, the fourth by the tensioner. Since the four runs formed a strand 1.674m. long, extremely accurate and effective tensioning was essential. The Morse tensioner had a nylon shoe approximately 280mm. long so the force per unit area on the shoe was small, avoiding undue noise and wear. Nylon offered a low co-efficient of friction and high temperature resistance, and its flexibility increased with temperature so that when the engine was warm the shoe readily conformed to changes in the shape of the chain run throughout its life. A special one-way 'anti-backlash' device was incorporated in the tie that held the shoe in the bowed condition to ensure that the chain could not possibly go slack in the event of backfire or suchlike.

Camshaft timing could be set through venier adjustment while valve timing was, inlet 17 degrees b.t.d.c., 59 degrees a.b.d.c.; exhaust, 59 degrees b.b.d.c., 17 degrees a.t.d.c. The firing order was 1 - 12 - 5 - 8 - 3 - 10 - 6 - 7 - 2 - 11 - 4 - 9 with the banks numbered front to back, o/s first. The ignition employed a single distributor driven from the cast iron jackshaft running in steel backed white metal bearings in the vee. The distributor fired 14mm. Champion N9Y plugs. The coil was a Lucas oil-filled item while the engine was started by a Lucas pre-engaged starter from a Lucas battery. A Butec alternator was belt driven via twin vee-belts from the front of the crankshaft.

A centrifugal impeller-type water pump was also belt driven from the crank nose, the one pump feeding both banks. The three-branch inlet manifolds were water heated, while oil cooling was by an oil : water heat exchanger. This was located beneath the shallow front portion of the sump and was claimed to drop oil temperature by 22 degrees centigrade for a one degree rise in the temperature of the water returning from the radiator. The oil pump was of the "crescent" gear-type and thus did not require an extra drive, since it could be keyed directly to the crankshaft. The extremely short pump was fitted between the front main bearing and the front wall of the crankcase and its pinion was splined on a sleeve which in turn was keyed to the crankshaft.

For the Series III E-type the V12 was fitted with three into two into one exhaust pipes and with all ancillaries (including electric pumps to supply the twin Strombergs) and emission equipment weight was quoted as 680lb. The pioneering V12 model made it entrance early in 1971 and was followed in 1972 by Jaguar's first V12-engined saloon, the

XJ12, later made available in two door coupe form. The E-type was phased out in 1975, the year which brought the XJ-S Gran Tourismo coupe based on familiar XJ mechanicals and equipped with Bosch designed, Lucas developed electronic fuel injection for improved fuel economy.

Fuel economy was also reasoning behind an 'HE' version of the engine introduced in mid 1981, HE standing for high efficiency. This version employed the so called May Fireball combustion chamber, developed by Swiss engineering genius Michael May - the first man to run a wing on a racing car, back in 1956. May had helped Ferrari pioneer Bosch mechanical indirect fuel injection in the world of Grand Prix racing and later assisted BMW's pioneering turbocharged racing saloon. Announced in 1976, his Fireball combustion chamber was designed specifically for road application and was fitted to the regular Jaguar V12 engine with merely some recalibration of the fuel injection system and some modifications to the ignition system.

The May chamber was designed to burn very weak mixtures for high thermal efficiency and reduced exhaust emissions. With plenty of air present the formation of CO was discouraged while piston crown temperature was kept relatively low allowing a small top land clearance, this further helping reduce hydrocarbon emissions which tend to be generated by quenching of flame in such clearances. Further, with lower peak combustion chamber temperatures the generation of oxides of nitrogen was minimal.

To burn the weak mixture a high compression ratio was necessary and this in turn helped fuel economy. In addition, a controlled degree of turbulence to distribute the flame and a high energy spark to set the combustion off vigorously were called for. Rather than a flathead and dished piston crown, the May chamber exploited a flat top piston and a two-zone recess in the head. One zone took the form of a dished recess in which was the inlet valve while the other extended further up into the head and accommodated both the exhaust valve and the plug.

As the piston approached t.d.c. on the compression stroke it forced the mixture out of the inlet valve recess into a channel guiding it tangentially into the deeper exhaust valve recess. This generated a rapid swirling motion which would help spread the flame throughout the mixture. The plug reached into a small pocket adjacent to the passage between the two zones where it was sheltered from the blast of swirling gas yet was in a position so that fresh mixture from the inlet valve had been directed onto it. Thus, the high energy spark found ignitable mixture and there was time for it to develop a strong flame front without danger of being quenched by the turbulence. The necessary spark was delivered by a modified Lucas transistorised ignition system.

Jaguar offered a choice of standard or HE engines for its V12 cars of the Eighties, the XJ-12 and XJ-S.

# The Image Makers

Robert Charles Tullius went from helping sell Kodak products to helping sell Jaguar products. Right from its inception in 1965 his smartly presented Group 44 racing team operated as a promotional vehicle for other companies. Partner Brian Fuerstenau concentrated on the technical side while Tullius developed the commercial aspect. "We had to pay the bills. Having been a salesman I knew that a properly presented team with its own built-in marketing and PR could promote someone's product effectively. In those days that was a new concept", Tullius reflects.

Group 44 worked initially with Standard Triumph's importer and Quaker State oils and after the formation of BMC Tullius raced MG as well as Triumph sports cars. Although Group 44 concentrated on SCCA 'amateur' racing Tullius had ambitions as a professional driver and he won the first ever Trans Am race held in 1967 at Daytona in a Dodge Dart. In 1968 he joined the crew of the Howmet turbine car team at Le Mans. To one day take Group 44 to Le Mans was a dream, but surely not a practical ambition?

In 1974 Tullius persuaded the British Leyland importer to add the V12 Series III E-type to its SCCA programme and both Group 44 on the east coast and Huffaker Engineering on the west coast were supplied cars, parts and some funds, as usual. There was no direct communication between the teams and the factory and these days there was no official factory competition programme. The importer-backed SCCA cars contested regional championships and the annual national run-off. Both teams won regional titles with the E-types and Group 44 won the 1975 national accolade.

By the end of '75 stocks of the E-type were exhausted but Tullius managed to get agreement for an exploratory Trans Am outing with the V12 XJ-S in 1976. This was sufficiently encouraging for Group 44 to be granted a full Trans Am programme in 1977. It was felt that the XJ-S needed a more sporting image to sell strongly in the States. By this stage the factory was supporting a European Touring Car Championship bid, though for different marketing considerations that programme was employing the more cumbersome XJ-12 saloon. The Group 44 XJ-S found success, winning Trans Am titles in '77 and '78 whereas the Broadspeed run ETCC effort lost direction and ended prematurely, in disgrace.

After the '78 season the importer withdrew backing for the Trans Am effort: under British Leyland Jaguar was running into trouble. It didn't revive until it was freed from the shackles of nationalisation in 1980. The late Andrew Whyte, acclaimed Jaguar historian and former employee put it thus: "Jaguar's new chairman John Egan was beginning to put the spirit back into the old firm. For five years it had had to do without a real boss; firms go downhill quickly in those circumstances".

In the States the restructured Jaguar Cars Inc. operation shared the optimism. Marketing chief Michael Dale, an expatriate Briton, was a former Healey man and an SCCA Sprite racer and he had enthusiastically embraced Tullius' various racing projects throughout the Leyland years. Indeed, his enthusiasm for racing as a marketing tool had been a major impetus for the original E-type campaign. Dale was confident Group 44 could do a first class job for Jaguar on any level and welcomed Tullius' bold suggestion that the newly independent Jaguar fund a GTP programme with long term Le Mans potential. IMSA GTP and Group C were exciting new categories emerging from the Le Mans GTP category of the late Seventies and looked set to revitalise international sports car racing.

Although it was early days, it was anticipated that the Jaguar V12 engine, which had been developed to give over 550b.h.p. in Trans Am guise, should be competitive under the published IMSA GTP and perhaps also Group C regulations. IMSA GTP offered sliding scales balancing weight and displacement for various types of engine while Group C was based around a limited quantity of fuel with engine choice free. Though chassis regulations also differed, Tullius was able to build a sports-prototype chassis that would be eligible for both categories.

Tullius' plan for an IMSA GTP car with long term Le Mans ambitions was well timed. Jaguar's new regime appreciated that the company's rich Le Mans heritage had done much to make its reputation and agreed that the time had come for the company to aim to revive that tradition. Dale calculated that to fund Group 44's enticing project

*The prototype of the Group 44 XJR-5 started running in 1982. In 1984 the IMSA GTP car took Jaguar back to Le Mans as a challenger for overall victory for the first time since the Fifties.*

would mean selling 200 more Jaguars a year in the USA. Typifying the new spirit he resolved to find a way.

Dale's philosophy was that to undertake something as ambitious as an IMSA GTP programme would play down the company's problems and suggest to the rest of the world that things were brighter than they actually were in cold commercial terms at this time. Egan's primary concerns were presenting the best possible image for the newly independent company and carrying on its traditions. The Group 44 project would do both.

As an interim measure, Group 44 was granted a Trans Am programme in 1981, again with the XJ-S. At the end of that very competitive season Tullius was able to remark: "I'd got to the stage of disbanding Group 44 as a racing team , then the effect of John Egan's arrival at Coventry began to be reflected over here. I'd worked with Mike Dale for years - he was quite a racer himself in SCCA - and he knew our capabilities. We were given some rope in 1981 and we didn't hang ourselves. We'd begun to do well again and so had Jaguar. From those factors came acceptance of our GTP project".

In the meantime Jaguar Cars Inc. had entirely funded the GTP car design phase and for 1982 Egan gave the green light for the importer to back an IMSA Camel GT race programme commencing in midseason. Jaguar was now well on the road to recovery, greatly assisted by improving sales in the USA. A small amount of additional backing

would come from long time supporter Quaker State (and Tullius now had a Quaker State distributorship) while Tullius also received assistance from Goodyear.

The GTP car was the design of freelancer Lee Dykstra whom Tullius had met back in the Sixties when he was racing the Dodge and Dykstra was a project engineer on the Ford Trans Am team. With the cessation of Ford racing activities in the Seventies Dykstra had been moved over to safety cars but weekends and evenings he started working with IMSA racer Al Holbert, helping develop Holbert's Chevrolet Monza. In '79 Dykstra and Holbert worked on a spaceframe Can Am car run by Hogan Racing and for 1980 Holbert established his own team and Dykstra formed the Grand Rapids, Michigan agency 'Special Chassis Inc.' which designed a state of the art ground effect machine for it.

Holbert's CAC-1 was extremely successful and early in 1981 Tullius asked Dykstra to submit a design and cost proposal for a ground effect GTP chassis specifically with long term Le Mans potential. Terms were quickly agreed and Dykstra spent much of '81 running wind tunnel tests. The alloy monocoque chassis was constructed at the Winchester, Virginia base of Group 44 under the direction of Lawton 'Lanky' Foushee who had succeeded Fuerstenau as engineering director, Fuerstenau having set up a freelance agency that undertook many projects for Group 44. Foushee was a one-time Air Force One engineer (tending the presidential jet) who had worked in NASCAR before joining Group 44 as Crew Chief in the early Seventies.

The engine for the new prototype was lifted from the '81 Trans Am car. Thus, it retained stock (ported) two valve single cam heads. However, Trans Am rules offered plenty of scope for tuning and the V12 had been permitted to run with six Weber carburettors. Well honed, Group 44's 5343cc. Trans Am power plant produced in the region of 570 b.h.p. on high octane racing fuel, running to 8,000 r.p.m. Engine development was undertaken in house, the work directed by John Huber.

Chassis and engine were mated in the spring of '82 and the so called 'XJR-5' (following the SCCA E-type and three generations of Trans Am XJ-S) first ran at the local Summit Point circuit on June 21 and 25. It then ran at Road Atlanta in early July, showing an encouraging turn of speed after which it was put in the nearby Lockheed wind tunnel, recording a cd figure of 0.38. In late July Jaguar Engineering Chief Jim Randle flew out from the UK to watch it testing at Road America and couldn't find a serious flaw in the project. He reported to Egan: "(Group 44) are a great bunch...so adaptable and so very competent, and a credit to the name of Jaguar; to reach such a standard, this quickly, really is an achievement".

Tullius and co-driver Bill Adam had run a simulated race at Road America and Egan flew out himself to see the debut race at the same circuit the following month. Tullius finished a highly creditable third, two laps down on the winning GTX Porsche 935 but winning GTP - "who could ask for more?" remarked Egan. Sadly, a shunt in qualifying at Mid Ohio early in September upset the momentum, causing the team to miss not only the Mid Ohio race but also that at Road Atlanta. Tullius only got two more races in '82. The V12 suffered terminal vibration at Pocono then the XJR-5 was one of many flat tyre victims at the Daytona IMSA finale, Tullius hitting the wall.

1982 had always been slated as a development year: 1983 would be the year Jaguar would first seriously challenge for GTP honours. 1983 found Group 44 entirely sponsored by Jaguar. In Europe the factory was officially backing the Tom Walkinshaw Racing ETCC bid. Jaguar was back in racing in a way that it hadn't been since the pre-merger days of the XK engine.

The '83 IMSA season started with the gruelling Daytona 24 and Sebring 12 hour races sandwiching a washed-out Miami sprint. The rugged GTX category Porsche 935 dominated both endurance events. At Daytona Tullius/Adam suffered suspension failure following a broken wheel bearing while at Sebring a head gasket went. However, Tullius/Adam took control of the following 500km. race at Road Atlanta to give Jaguar its first Camel GT win. The series then moved to California where over two weekends Holbert took charge of the points table driving a Chevrolet-March. Tullius crashed on oil at

Riverside then finished second at Laguna Seca.

For the balance of the season Holbert was able to switch to a brand new Porsche-March and Tullius had his work cut out to try and cut the points deficit. The Porsche engine was a 3.2 litre turbo developed by ace American tuner Alvin Springer to produce in excess of 700 b.h.p. in spite of running air cooled two valve, single plug heads while the March chassis was every bit as advanced as the Jaguar ground effect design and both packages weighed in at around 925kg. With less than 600 b.h.p. on tap the Jaguar was frequently outrun. There was also a continuing head gasket weakness to be overcome. Nevertheless, with good stamina Tullius took two more victories with co-driver Adam, then yet another sharing with Harry 'Doc' Bundy.

Mid season, Group 44 had missed a race at Daytona to allow the XJR-5 to be shipped to the UK for a test at Silverstone. This took place in late June, after Le Mans, with Rothmans Porsche 956 driver Derek Bell at the wheel. Porsche was happy for its works driver to give his comments to Coventry, mindful of the need for a more competitive World Endurance Championship. The series had become a procession of 956 cars. The test went well and was, in effect, the first step towards Le Mans for Group 44.

Back home, more power was clearly required to answer the Porsche-March challenge and for 1984 Group 44 planned a 6.0 litre engine, increasing dimensions from 90.0 x 70.0mm. to 90.0 x 78.0mm. This would have engine management for improved economy and driveability - both important Le Mans considerations, of course. Jaguar had been encouraged by the four '83 wins and Tullius' runner up position in the Camel GT title chase and Group 44 was able to expand to two cars. Again, an important consideration if it was to go to France...

Le Mans veteran Brian Redman announced the third comeback of a long and distinguished career to take the lead role in the second car, Adam having quit. Bundy and Pat Bedard would be the co-drivers. Redman's recruitment was announced in December '83 and he immediately began testing the 6.0 litre 'electronic' engine with its Micos engine management system at Daytona. It had been under development since August and, if successful, would be the engine to take Jaguar back to the scene of former glories.

Tullius, of course, wanted to go to Le Mans above all and following the full season of GTP racing with the carburettor engine equipped prototype XJR-5 he felt Group 44 was ready. While Jaguar Cars Inc. guided the GTP programme, a Le Mans bid had to be the decision of the parent company. Coventry did not rule it out for '84: if the Daytona 24 Hour race went well Le Mans preparations could be made...

Daytona went reasonably well. The cars were fast - and 220 m.p.h. on the banking promised competitive speed on the Mulsanne - and were again shown to be basically sound. However, there

were niggling problems for both entries throughout the 24 hour race. During the course of the meeting Tullius met Le Mans race director Alain Bertaut and told the French press: "the ACO isn't normally very hospitable towards American teams but Bertaut reassured me on that point".

Bertaut was in a group of European motor racing politicians visiting Daytona. The ACO was keen to attract American entries; FISA was concerned at the Porsche take-over of Group C and looked enviously at the greater diversity in IMSA GTP. Soon after Daytona FISA announced changes to Group C regulations aimed at bringing them closer to GTP. Firstly it would scrap the published tighter fuel allowance for '84 - even though Porsche and Lancia had been working towards this over the winter - and would raise the minimum weight to 850kg. Then for '85 it would introduce IMSA-type sliding scales relating weight to engine type and displacement in place of the fuel formula.

Ironically, the apparent sell-out to IMSA did not suit Jaguar: the envisaged scales gave the Porsche Group C engine a greater potential at 2.5 litres than the 3.2 litre GTP engine already had. Yet Porsche likewise could not find favour with the new moves, having worked to published regulations having been promised stability. It announced a Le Mans boycott by its factory team in protest. On the other hand Jaguar felt that participation at Le Mans would give it a voice in the argument.

In the short term the 850kg. Group C minimum weight would help lessen the disadvantage of the over-900kg. XJR-5 at Le Mans. It was felt that with a continuing 2600 litre fuel ration the Group C turbocars would race with around 650b.h.p. and the 6.0 litre electronic engine was not far off matching that, in spite of a lower compression ratio in view of the mandatory lower octane fuel. Soon after the third and 24th place finishes at Daytona came a magnificent one - two at Miami, a triumph beamed to TV viewers around the world. Jaguar was back on the international stage.

The entry for Le Mans was made in March 1984 as required by the regulations but participation was to be conditional upon the success of a race simulation at Pocono in May. The Pocono trial meant missing IMSA races but Jaguar and Group 44 were serious about their Le Mans intentions. Prior to Pocono Claude Ballot-Lena, a veteran of a record 18 Le Mans starts, was drafted into the Le Mans effort and he had his first taste of the XJR-5 at the Pennsylvanian circuit.

Pocono was chosen for its combination of a high speed 2.5 mile tri-oval with an 0.3 mile infield road course but busy circuit schedules meant that Group 44 could only have use from 4.0pm. on May 10 and from 2.0pm. the following day. Consequently, the exercise was split into two runs with only routine pitstop maintenance between. On hand to drive with Ballot-Lena were Tullius and Bundy while Dale and Randle represented the decision makers.

A brand new XJR-5 was wheeled out for the trial, this the fourth chassis prepared in '84. There were

*A dream come true for Robert Charles Tullius: his own car at Le Mans. Tullius had previously competed at the wheel of a Howmet turbine car. The XJR-5 was more conventional and more significant.*

a few new car gremlins - such as a defective starter and a loose screw that caused a brake caliper to lose grease - but that was only to be expected since there had been no prior shake-down for the chassis. The car ran so sweetly throughout the night that the first run was extended to 15 hours from the planned 12. The only worry was a herd of deer that apparently had a habit of grazing on the infield at night: Bundy glanced one of the creatures but fortunately both parties escaped intact from the hair-raising experience.

The remaining nine hours were run off with little bother other than a stripped third gear. In the light of that stronger gears were specified. The Micos engine functioned perfectly - important since the electronic engine was needed for a serious Le Mans bid - and Tullius remarked that the test had fulfilled expectations: "any inadequacies which turned up were easily fixed and were primarily due to using a brand new car".

Randle's report was guardedly optimistic: "with further attention to points of detail the cars should stand up to the special demands of the 24 hours at Le Mans. The last three hours were run at considerably higher speed without ill effects. There were some unscheduled stops, but none that would have put the car out of contention in a race... Group 44's cars are well designed and well prepared and the name of Jaguar can only be enhanced by their presence".

A few days later Egan gave the green light. In the words of Jim Randle: "we recognise that our return to Le Mans for the first time since our five victories in the Fifties will be a learning exercise. Although we have no realistic chance of winning, I know Bob Tullius and the Group 44 team will be trying hard to produce a creditable result". Or, as Dale put it: "we'll settle for having cars that run well and finish. The development benefits that participation can give us are what we want".

Late May brought an IMSA race at Charlotte and Group 44 ran two cars in this to keep faith with IMSA, having missed two races in California due to the Pocono test. Meanwhile, back at base the XJR-5 total was increased to five cars with two race cars plus a new spare prepared for shipment to France. The drivers in France were to be Tullius/ Bundy/Redman in car 44 while Ballot-Lena shared 40 with new recruit John Watson and Tony Adamowicz, the latter replacing Bedard who was injured at Indianapolis. Of the six drivers, only 35 year old Bundy and 37 year old Watson were under 40. Tullius put a premium on experience and caution.

The Micos-engined XJR-5s ran essentially in Daytona trim, with additional cooling ducts for the gearbox, and weighed in at around 930kg. Although Porsche was absent as a factory team it dominated the opposition with no less than 16 customer cars and teams of the calibre of Joest Racing, Kremer Racing, John Fitzpatrick Racing and Richard Lloyd Racing. Chief rivals were three works Lancias while the normally aspirated entry was headed by Group 44 and Aston Martin Downe, the latter running two cars. Immaculately presented as always, the XJR-5s were given the rare privilege of a spacious paddock area and were hugely impressive to European eyes.

Tullius imposed a 6,450r.p.m. rev limit for qualifying and gave strict instructions to his drivers to proceed cautiously and not to endanger the cars in any way. Bundy had a spin at the Ford chicane and knocked the nose off 44 but that was the only incident. The team concentrated on getting gearing and springing right and the cars were timed at a best of 216.8m.p.h. on the Mulsanne - just a whisker off the computer-predicted 217m.p.h.! However, there was a tendency to wander on the unique straight so a little more wing was added. This also improved stability in the corners, which had been less than perfect.

Redman clocked 3m. 35.33s. to put 44 on the seventh row, 14th fastest, while Watson recorded 3m. 39.16s. in 40 - just inside the top 20 - after water in the cylinders had necessitated an engine swap then a Micos system problem had needed rectifying. By way of comparison, the pole time - from a sticky tyre shod, highly boosted Lancia - was 3m. 17.11s. while the best Porsche privateer recorded 3m. 26.10s. Mallock slipped qualifying tyres onto the Aston Martin Downe to record 3m. 33.12s, much to Aston Martin's delight.

Nevertheless, Jaguar got the biggest applause when the cars were wheeled out onto the grid. The team's basic strategy was to run consistently until daylight on Sunday, then for 40 to charge while 44 continued to motor carefully to the finish. Hopefully, in the meantime the turbo car entry would have wilted. If Jaguar had an advantage it was in time between refuelling stops: Group 44 was hoping to run just over sixty minutes whereas the turbos would refuel well before the hour mark. In the event, with its additional downforce Group 44 found itself averaging around 57 minutes compared to around 48 minutes for the turbos. Of course, the first hour was run, as usual, at a faster pace and the leaders started coming in after 40 minutes. Tullius was able to go on for 55 minutes and for one glorious lap led the Vingt Quatre Heures du Mans...

The Jaguars settled down keeping four to eight seconds a lap in hand yet were well established in the top ten. At three hours car 40 was sixth a couple of laps down, car 44 12th yet on the same lap. The six hour mark found the cars sixth and seventh, running in close company with the Mallock Aston Martin Downe. Alas, shortly afterwards the entire Aston Martin team was wiped out in a horrifying high speed accident at the Mulsanne kink which claimed the life of a track marshal. The pace cars were out for around an hour, saving fuel which the turbo cars could put to good effect later...

The Jaguars continued to hold sixth and seventh positions on the same lap until midnight when Adamowicz brought 40 in with a chunked tyre, dropping to eighth. Then at around 3.00am., half distance, Ballot-Lena radioed in to report a broken throttle cable. He was instructed to rig up a repair using the spare on board, without falling foul of the regulations by accepting outside assistance. He successfully got the car back to the pits and the entire incident cost eight laps. An hour later a deflating tyre caught Adamowicz: the XJR-5 had no tyre pressure monitor and the car went off unexpectedly at Terte Rouge, mercifully just ahead of the dauntingly fast Mulsanne. High speed on the Mulsanne tends to keep a deflating tyre up through centrifugal force but as soon as cornering forces go through the tyre at the flat out kink...

Adamowicz caught the barrier head on then rebounded to crunch the right side of the car. Nevertheless, he was able to coax it back to the pits. Alas, the oil tank had been ruptured and the engine was on the point of seizing...

Car 44 was still running strongly and at 6.00am. still lay sixth. Sadly, just over an hour later came its first serious unscheduled stop. Just as at Pocono, third gear had stripped. The fault had been wrongly diagnosed. Repairing the gearbox took 46 minutes and dropped the car to 10th position. However, there was still hope of a strong finish and by 10.00am. the car was back in the top six. Just before 11.30am. Redman felt the gear change stiffen as he slowed for the Ford chicane on the approach to the pits. Unable to find second or third gear he swept into the pits. The gearbox had overheated and it was assumed that debris from the broken third gear had blocked an oilway.

The car was still a runner but there was no sure way of removing all the debris that might be present. The risk of gearbox seizure was high and clearly could have serious consequences. Jaguar could not risk an accident. Car 44 was pushed back to the paddock: a sad end to a fine showing.

Unpredictably, back home the 1984 Camel GT Championship was won by Randy Lanier in the Blue Thunder Chevrolet-March. Holbert took time to get the late arriving customer Porsche 962 up to speed and Group 44 had taken a lot of time out to contest Le Mans. By mid season Lanier had amassed a solid points advantage.

Daytona had started well enough for Group 44 with Tullius third on the grid, headed only by the ex-Holbert Kreepy Krauly team Porsche-March and the prototype 962, having a one-off race as a factory car with Andretti father and son at the controls. Running a 2.85 litre engine, the 962 was the swiftest car in the race but early on hit transmission trouble leaving Tullius and co. to fight it out with the South African drivers in the ex-Holbert car. Although still on carburettors unlike its sister car, the Jaguar could run further between stops and looked very strong, leading just over a hundred laps before hit by a spate of alternator drive belt failures. Three such breakages cost a total of 28 laps to the winning 83G. The 04 sister car lost over two hours following water pump drive problems.

Then came Miami and the terrific finish, Redman's 04 car leading Tullius' 44 over the line by just 81 seconds. The experimental Micos engine was working well for both cars which finished the three hour race on one fuel stop, which helped keep the opposition at bay.

Fired by his triumph, Redman claimed pole at Sebring and led the first lap - before Tullius took over, to command the first quarter of the 12 hour marathon. Then the troubles began, and they culminated in a terminal fuel system failure. Car 04 was also struck by gremlins - mainly ignition - and finished out of the picture. It was back in the frame at Road Atlanta but here Blue Thunder served notice of intent with a one-two finish for its Chevrolet-Marches. Redman finished third, a lap down while 44 finished 33rd after an incident befell Bundy...

After Road Atlanta Redman still headed the points chase, then the Le Mans programme took its toll. Jaguar skipped Riverside and Laguna Seca where Blue Thunder again came out on top. The 962 arrived as a customer car in California but didn't look as strong as at Daytona. Group 44 came back to bag second and third at Charlotte, a circuit not unlike Daytona where the Holbert/Bell 962 had looked on course for victory number one before its late retirement handed Blue Thunder another win.

Le Mans took Group 44 away for another two races, which saw victory for Kreepy Krauly then the 962, Bell at the wheel. It had taken the 3.2 litre engine to get the Porsche competitive as an all round contender. Jaguar was now set to return to the Camel trail but with Lanier runner up both times in its absence he now had over twice as many points as Redman, Group 44's highest scorer, and over half as many again as Bell, the best placed Porsche driver.

Holbert/Bell won at Watkins Glen with Redman/ Hurley Haywood (replacing Bedard) third but way behind after problems and car 44 on the sidelines. However, at Portland Tullius was leading with two laps to run... then a stop for a splash of fuel let Lanier through to win by a frustrating six seconds. This time car 40's problems dropped it to eighth. For the Sears Point one hour thrash Group 44's highest scorers Redman and Bundy took the two cars to second and third - to Whittington's Blue Thunder.

Holbert/Bell swept to success at Road America and Pocono, having really found form and setting a blistering pace in a last minute bid for the title. However, problems at Michigan and Watkins Glen handed the crown to surprise-champion Lanier. Meantime, Group 44 had found the Porsche pace punishing as rear suspension and drivetrain problems - in particular, c.w.p. failures - hurt reliability. The Hewland gearbox was now marginal for the power and torque of the 6.0 litre V12. The XJR-5 could only look to fuel economy and that factor saw the cars move into the hunt once more at the Daytona finale. Bundy was leading after his second stop when he crashed at the chicane, losing fifth place in the points table. Holbert/Bell won but Redman/Haywood finished second which left Redman sixth in the points standing, the highest placed Group 44 driver.

One of the '84 XJR-5 chassis was displayed at the 1984 Birmingham Motor Show and was subsequently kept in the UK where it was tested by TWR, Jaguar's ETCC XJ-S team, fitted with a four valve engine developed in Coventry. This engine had a 6.0 litre capacity, not applicable to IMSA but perfectly legal in Group C since the envisaged radical revision of regulations along IMSA lines had been shelved. Jaguar was now planning to go Group C as well as IMSA, and in 1985 would enter cars for Le Mans on behalf of both Group 44 and TWR.

Having run the four valve XJR-5, TWR convinced Jaguar that it should produce its own chassis for Group C and this would not appear before August '85. Meanwhile, Tullius was given the resources to contest both Le Mans and the Camel GT Championship without having to miss rounds, and to work towards a replacement for the existing car. Dykstra was continuing to refine the established design and over the winter of '84/'85 it underwent a fundamental change, receiving elements of the projected replacement model including a revised bellhousing, gearbox and underbody.

Continuing work with the Micos system had opened up the way to intake and exhaust modifications which provided more power and torque. With technical back up from Coventry, the 6.0 litre electronic engine had been developed for 1985 to produce around 650 b.h.p. on the high octane fuel permitted by IMSA. Huber's best '85 engine offered 670 b.h.p. which represented a 100 b.h.p. improvement since 1981 and that was backed by an extra 100 lb. ft. torque thanks to the increased capacity, work on the flow characteristics of the heads and the intake and exhaust improvements allowed by the Micos system.

The revised '85 XJR-5 was reckoned to be two seconds a lap quicker around Daytona. Again this season Group 44 would run two cars, Chip Robinson, a young Super Vee driver, coming in to replace Bundy alongside Tullius in 44 while Redman/Haywood again drove 40. This year Ballot-Lena and Jim Adams were the third drivers for Le Mans. At Le Mans the 1985 fuel ration was 2210 litres, which could be expected to slow the Porsches somewhat. Porsche was still the major rival on both sides of the Atlantic with two new March based turbo cars further potential threats. At Le Mans a 3.0 litre V6 Nissan-March promised high horsepower, as in IMSA did a 3.4 litre V6 Buick-March. However, few would bet on Porsche being toppled by Jaguar, Lancia or anyone else in 1985...

The revised, '85 XJR-5 warmed up for Le Mans with IMSA "qualifying times and finishing record satisfactory for Le Mans" as Tullius put it. That translates as two fourth place finishes, two third place finishes, four second places finishes and one

win from the eight races leading up to the French foray. In the face of more powerful Porsches and a more powerful Buick-March the team was again giving a good account of itself.

Dykstra's improved suspension made the '85 car - Jaguar called it the 'Phase II' XJR-5 - more stable in the corners and with the well developed electronic engine and experience of the special demands of the Le Mans circuit, hopes were high for a strong showing. Particularly given the 2,210 litre race ration and less weight this year. Tullius made it clear that his objective was to win. The two Group 44 cars were again Jaguar's only representatives, TWR awaiting its own car prior to starting its prototype programme. Strength in numbers is invaluable at Le Mans and Group 44 didn't have that.

Group 44 again took essentially standard trim chassis to La Sarthe and the improved stability was such that Redman reported that he could take the notorious flat out kink on either side of the road. This year the cars ran 7,500r.p.m. in practice and in first practice lapped 2.5 seconds faster than in 1984, again not pushing for times since the turbo cars had such an advantage.

Alas, when the serious business began on Wednesday night the team ran into a worrying detonation problem. The cars had first been fuelled prior to scrutineering: hence excessive weights on the ACO scales of around 1000kg. During the break in Wednesday qualifying fresh fuel was taken on from the mandatory ACO supply and both engines were lost that Wednesday night.

All the signs pointed to the quality of fuel taken on board. The ACO supply is notorious. Naturally the compression ratio had been reduced in anticipation of the lower octane factor and it couldn't be further altered. The team had to cautiously back its timing off to the detriment of fuel economy. During the course of the meeting the quality of the fuel supply appeared to improve again but the team dared not run its timing back again - it only had four engines.

This year the cars lined up 16th and 17th on the grid, three places behind the Aston Martin-EMKA which took over the role of normally aspirated pace setter from the absent Aston Martin Downe team. Otherwise, ahead were two Lancias and a dozen Porsches. The Lancia was a much revised car with new aerodynamics, cooling and weight distribution and was now running on Michelin tyres. It promised to be a real threat to Porsche. Tullius wanted another strong first hour showing for Jaguar but a vibration problem demanded caution. It turned out only to be a lost weight putting a wheel out of balance. Rather, the Needell Aston Martin-EMKA took the first hour initiative and a short lived lead - but only by running the first half an hour on light tanks then getting off the general fuel schedule with a quick stop to keep it going through the first proper stops!

Under normal circumstances revs creep up during a long race as the engine loosens but Group 44 kept its cars under 7,000r.p.m., on a tight leash. Careful driving and leaning the engines off helped reduce consumption from an initial 4.2 miles per gallon to 4.6. Neither car featured in the midnight top ten and *Motor Sport* was moved to comment: "We'd hoped to see the British backed cars doing better on fuel consumption, attacking, pressuring, going ahead when the Porsches and Lancias refuelled, as the 1985 regulations seemingly allowed them to do. In that respect they were disappointing, for their fuelling schedules were the same as those of the turbo teams, and they just lacked the pace to worry the opposition..."

It came back to the detonation danger - and the fact that the turbo cars were going more quickly than they were expected to on 2,210 litres, the Joest and Richard Lloyd cars setting a pace that embarrassed even the Porsche factory team. Jaguar's showing was made the painful by the fact that the Aston Martin-EMKA was running ahead of it, on the verge of the top ten on a fraction of the budget...

Worse was in store. Just after midnight car 40 (Redman/Haywood/Adams) coasted to a halt just beyond the pits, a c.v. joint broken. Resourcefully, Adams isolated the half shaft but having parked in a dangerous positions the officials had asked him to keep the car's lights on. The battery did not half enough juice left to re-start the engine.

Car 44 (Tullius/Robinson/Ballot-Lena) continued to run steadily, albeit behind the Aston Martin-EMKA and still outside the top ten. Then midway through Sunday morning it struck a misfire and lost 40 minutes through changes of Micos ECUs and throttle sensors. It transpired that there had been a point at which the throttle sensor wasn't making contact, and the first replacement sensor had the same problem...

With the final 90 minutes still to run and a top ten finish now in sight thanks to the general level of attrition, the car dropped a valve. A valve spring retainer had broken: the valve fell into the cylinder and a small portion of it actually punched clean through the cylinder head.

Group 44 didn't give up, tackling the tricky job of trying to isolate the damage to allow the car to limp home. The cylinder had to be filled with liquid rubber: after 15 minutes setting time this held the debris in place. The valves then had to be deactivated - by breaking the camshaft with a hammer and chisel! Finally, the injection system was isolated and with the plug left out car 44 was ready to limp home on 11 cylinders. It ran so well that Tullius drove the lap a little too quickly and thus had to complete two laps to be able to see the flag and collect the 13th place classification. Unlucky for some.

Back home, the unlucky story of the 1985 Camel GT Championship had been told in the first round, as usual the 24 hours of Daytona. There were six 962 privateer cars and the model dominated, a brief challenge from a Buick V6-March fizzling out

early on. Under 1985 IMSA rules Jaguar was the underdog. Nevertheless, Tullius/Redman/Haywood got the 44 car well into the hunt... until 11.00pm. At that point Tullius had a spectacular shunt caused by tyre deflation as he exited the chicane powering towards the East banking. The car caught fire, its bodywork began to deform and Tullius couldn't get the door open. He tore off his helmet to put his head through the window for fear of suffocation and having ripped his gloves off so as to act faster he suffered minor burns to his hands.

The sister car fared little better, retiring with zero oil pressure. At Miami Tullius/Robinson in 44 suffered transmission failure while Redman/Haywood hit the wall and lost a lap, finishing fourth. At Sebring it was the turn of 44 to finish fourth, after hitting a tyre wall and losing 20 laps: 04 suffered engine failure. But at Road Atlanta 04 came through to win ahead of 44 after the quickest 962 and the Buick-March had been delayed. That was the high point of the season: Jaguar had to hope for Porsche failures and didn't see the winner's circle again. Even with 670b.h.p. it was well short of Porsche and Buick horsepower. Its only advantage was its considerable and instantly on tap torque: its turbo lagged rivals found heavy traffic harder going.

Car 44 finished third at Riverside... where Redman had been leading in 04 when he was rudely punted off by a backmarker. Car 44 finished second at Laguna Seca, where 04 finished third. 04 went on to finish second at Charlotte after a broken seat belt buckle cost the lead and second at Lime Rock where another likely win was lost to the fact that Redman's windscreen become so badly obscured by oil that he had to open the door to find the pit road! Car 44 finished third at Mid Ohio, then 04 finished fourth at Watkins Glen, then 44 finished second at Portland... without threatening Holbert's winning Porsche. The post Le Mans performances were less convincing. Car 04 finished second at Pocono, where Holbert came from behind with his superior horsepower to take the lead five laps from the finish. He ran home to the Camel GT title amid talk of IMSA slowing the 962 - the regulations clearly gave the two valve turbo engine too much scope.

At Watkins Glen 04 took third, then it was second in the Daytona finale. Daytona brought the long awaited 'XJR-7': essentially a 'Phase II' XJR-5 with a new, composite monocoque. Debuted by Tullius and Robinson, it finished a solid fourth. The new car would run the '86 season leaving the overall tally for the XJR-5 as six wins, 14 second places and 12 thirds from three seasons.

Meanwhile, TWR had been granted a full World Endurance Championship programme which commenced at Mosport in August '85. Through '86 TWR ran Group C and carried forward Jaguar's Le Mans aspirations while Group 44 concentrated upon GTP. In '86 the American team was able to go to 6.5 litres, increasing its bore to 94mm., albeit at

*Group 44 returned to Le Mans in 1985 with high hopes but the XJR-5 could not find competitive speed. Racing a GTP car in the French classic turned out to be a heavy handicap for American team.*

However, Group 44 managed two further victories in '87. That was somewhat ironic since the team only had finance for a part season. And it subsequently lost the IMSA contract to TWR which was finding great success in Group C. Before exploring the TWR V12 prototypes which paved the path to World Championship and Le Mans glory, we shall take a closer look at the Group 44 Le Mans car.

# XJR-5

As we have noted, the Group 44 GTP engine was a direct development of the team's earlier production racer V12 engine. The first E-type had rolled out with a blueprinted engine, prepared under the direction of Fuerstenau. It had boasted ported and polished heads, heavy duty valve springs, reground cams, racing pistons and rings running in carefully honed liners, lightened and balanced con rods but essentially a stock crank. Ignition was CD utilising the standard distributor while the flywheel was a lightweight aluminium item run with a racing clutch and the oil system was modified wet sump. High octane racing fuel, an 11.0:1 compression ratio and the team's own six-into-one exhaust system released 460 b.h.p. on standard carburation. Early on the team introduced a dry sump but not much else could be done given the regulations. The Trans Am car, however, was allowed a six Weber carburettor set up to replace the standard fuel injection with which the XJ-S was equipped and which was not considered race worthy.

Developed by former Jaguar engineer Ron Beaty's Forward Engineering concern in the UK where it was sold as an aftermarket item, the six double choke Weber kit dramatically improved breathing. The Trans Am engine offered over 530 b.h.p. from the outset and with camshaft and porting work as permitted under Trans Am rules power rose to 570 b.h.p. on the high octane racing fuel permitted and an 8,000 r.p.m. rev limit was achieved. By 1981 thanks to lighter titanium valves, easier cam profiles, better valve springs and better valve cooling through increased oil splash 8,000 r.p.m. could be run throughout a six hour race rather than in short doses, as previously. Only for 12 and 24 hour races were revs reduced, to just below 7,000r.p.m.

For the GTP adventure this 5.3 litre carburettor engine now prepared by in house builder John Huber had merely received slight modifications to cylinder heads and auxiliary equipment. However, for 1984 a full 6.0 litre version was readied through production of a longer, 78mm. throw crankshaft. This took power over the 600b.h.p. mark. As we have noted, the other major development was an engine management system, still under development at the start of '84. This was commissioned by the factory from Lucas in Birmingham and was known as the Micos system

the expense of an additional 25 kilos. Group 44's bigger displacement engine was soon developed to provide 703b.h.p./7,250r.p.m. on a 12.8:1 compression ratio. Right at the end of '86 Group 44 slotted the 6.5 litre engine into its XJR-7 chassis and won the Daytona finale: its first success of the season.

As we have seen, the XJR-7 had arrived at the '85 Daytona finale in prototype form and was essentially an XJR-5 with a lightweight, rigid composite replacement tub. The tub, however, retained metal bulkheads. For the switch to the XJR-7 Group 44 had relocated some of the ancillaries on the front of its V12 engine for a shorter package and there was now only a single ancillary drivebelt. The rear suspension had been revised with a wider crossmember supporting more upright dampers but this arrangement had already been grafted onto the XJR-5.

The XJR-7 had gone into 1986 still equipped with a Hewland VG gearbox and both Daytona 24 hour entries suffered transmission woes. The 15kg. heavier, stronger VGC 'box did not arrive until late in the season. Early in the season Dykstra had fallen out with Tullius and had quit the team, which continued to play underdog to Porsche. Porsche's domination was in spite of the outlawing of the cockpit boost control and the imposition of an extra 72kg. handicap for 1986. In response to the 3.0 litre displacement limit of 1987, Porsche developed a revised engine taking advantage of the fact that it could introduce twin ignition and its Motronic engine management system. This was strong enough to continue the Porsche parade.

since it was produced by Lucas' Micos electronics division.

The Micos system controlled both ignition and injection. The ignition was still CD, in other words of the so called 'capacitor discharge' type, this using a condenser, or 'capacitor' in which to store electrical energy as it builds up. Such a system has similar triggering to a contactless coil system - such as Lucas Opus - but activating a thyristor condenser. The term thyristor indicates a switching device, while this condenser is another form of transistor capable of storing extremely high voltage and currents up to 100 amps. The capacitor supplies current to the coil at elevated voltage: the system incorporates capacitor charging and voltage amplifying circuits, the latter to increase voltage between the battery and the capacitor from around 12 volts to up to 250 volts. Since the CD spark kicks off from a much higher voltage a very high secondary voltage can be supplied to the spark plug. The system offers a higher energy, shorter duration spark.

With Micos, the injection was fully electronic. In the electronic system an ECU takes readings from a variety of engine sensors and activates triggers controlling solenoid-operated injectors, determining the timing and duration of of injection. The Micos system employed Bosch injectors and worked at around 5 bar. Early electronic injection systems had been developed by Bosch for road cars - a well known example its low pressure, analogue-based L-Jetronic system, introduced in 1973.

The early Eighties brought more sophisticated systems - such as Micos in which information from the sensors was converted from analogue to digital values by a digital converter to allow the ECU to incorporate a micro processor. A micro processor can cope with information from a great variety of sensors monitoring the engine's operating conditions: fuel pressure and temperature, air temperature, water temperature and battery voltage can be read, in addition to load (throttle position) and speed. Jaguar employed six such sensors, of which load and speed were by far the most important.

Crank angle was established by the sensors and injection and ignition timing could thus be set to relate to it. A low voltage pulse from the ECU triggered the servo motor/ injector drive and ignition amplifier to provide the optimum fuelling and ignition advance/retard for the conditions identified by the various sensors. The micro-processor, in essence, consisted of two chips: a RAM (Random Access Memory) chip to do the calculations and a plug-in EPROM (Erasable, Programmable, Read Only Memory) chip to dictate the ignition and injection settings appropriate to a given combination of sensor readings.

The various dictates form what is known as a map and are compiled as a result of extensive dynomometer testing. For example, a reading will be taken every 250r.p.m. for a given throttle

opening to determine optimum ignition and injection settings for those conditions of load and speed. Control of the settings will then be fine tuned by the ECU according to the other sensor readings and the basic laws of physics - for example, low water temperature indicates warm up and the fuelling will be richened accordingly.

Crucial to the whole system is the basic software - and patient dyno testing. The plug-in EPROM facility allows fine tuning of the map at the trackside. Originally the map will have been transferred from the main dyno computer and at the track the EPROM can be removed again from the ECU and plugged into a portable EPROM programmer for alteration. For example, major overrun cannot be simulated on the dyno but can be accommodated in the light of track experience.

Clearly the process of mapping on the dyno was exhaustive and on-going as engine specifications evolved. On the track, digital control, while not increasing top end power, offered, as we have suggested, better response and overall a more driveable engine. The challenge was to write software capable of doing the job without any 'bugs', to get the mapping right and, perhaps most important of all, to protect the micro processor's sophisticated circuits from interference. These circuits are highly sensitive to 'spikes' - interference in the form of electro-magnetic pulses generated mainly by the ignition system - calling for very careful location and insulation of the ECU and its wiring.

First tested at Daytona in December '83, the Micos system was very much an "experimental" development when first raced early in '84. While initially it provided better throttle response, with development it allowed the fuel consumption to be improved, an important consideration with a view to Le Mans where fuel was tightly restricted. In IMSA fuel was high octane, maximum tank capacity was 120 litres and these was no restriction on the number of times a competitor could refuel or on the total quantity a competitor could use. At Le Mans the organisers provided a mandatory 97/102 octane fuel supply, the maximum tank capacity was 100 litres and each competitor was rationed to so many litres for the 24 hour race.

Designed by Dykstra, the XJR-5 chassis taken to Le Mans in '84 followed on from a CRC-2 Can Am wing car design that had found much success in 1981. A roofed CRC-2 was the starting point for development of the overall XJR-5 shape while monocoque and suspension were developed from CRC technology. A key difference was the length of the engine block: the CRC had run a Chevrolet V8 whereas the XJR-5 had to accommodate a significantly longer unit. Further, it had to keep the driver's feet behind the front wheel axis to conform to GTP regulations and needed a centrally located fuel tank to meet Group C requirements. The wheelbase measured 108.5 inches/ 2743mm. compared to 104.5 inches/ 2650mm. for a Porsche 956.

A long wheelbase is not a disadvantage in itself. In theory, a long wheelbase car enjoys lower slip angles at which a given cornering force is generated and, all other things being equal, will be easier, more forgiving to drive. Further, it tends to improve a car's lift:drag ratio. And awkwardness in slow corners is something of a myth: even the famous 'Loewes (nee Station) Hairpin' at Monaco is not particularly tight compared to the length of a long wheelbase Grand Prix car, as Gordon Murray points out. Murray added a 75mm. spacer to his late Seventies Brabham BT49 chassis and it found over a second a lap, and was perfectly balanced everywhere.

Far more significant is weight distribution. The classic front:rear split is 40:60. More weight on the rear improves traction but understeer is an inherent danger. The problem of the Jaguar V12 engine was its length together with its considerable weight - well in excess of 200kg. compared to less than 150kg. for a typical aluminium racing engine such as the Cosworth DFV. As we have seen, Dykstra went for a wheelbase four inches longer than that of the contemporary Porsche 956 Group C car. Yet to keep the wheelbase within reasonable bounds the bellhousing was very short. In other words (running a conventional outboard Hewland gearbox) the XJR-5 set the rear of the weighty V12 block very close to the rear axle line.

At least the heavy engine was a rugged structure that could be run fully stressed. The rear suspension was supported by a tubular subframe bolted to the transaxle while the engine accepted additional stiffening struts running from the firewall bulkhead to the block and from the roll cage to the heads. Fabricated by Group 44, the aluminium monocoque had an aluminium honeycomb floor, steel tube reinforced bulkheads and integral mandatory alloy steel roll cage as stiffening members. Box members either side of the cockpit added further to structural rigidity.

The monocoque needed to be practical to build in the team's Winchester 'shop yet torsionally rigid in view of the downforce that could be expected from the harnessing of ground effect. Incorporating the central fuel tank and side pontoons, the tub extended from the firewall bulkhead to the front of the pedal box with the master cylinders projecting through the front wall and protected by a detachable nose box. The pedals reached back to the front axle line and a bulkhead at this point carried front suspension supports and and the steering rack. The steering rack and pinion was by Schroeder - later Jack Knight - and the rack was positioned just ahead of the front wheel axis and was accessed via a detachable plate in the top of the pedal box.

Front and rear suspension were conventional with unequal length upper and lower wishbones, Koni co-axial coil spring/dampers and anti roll bar. At the rear the Koni units, although operated directly by the uprights, were mounted high over the transaxle a subframe supporting them. This subframe was positioned over the two transaxle crossmembers which supported the top wishbones. The lower wishbone mounts were positioned at the base of the transaxle case. The lower wishbones were wide based with the forward mount at the bellhousing, the rear mount at the rear of the gearbox.

Positioning the dampers above the uprights allowed diffuser tunnels to pass through the rear suspension with the minimum of obstruction. Dykstra incorporated large diffuser tunnels. Burdened with a flat bottom area of 800mm. x 1000mm. to conform to Group C regulations, and with sliding skirts illegal Dykstra treated the entire cockpit floor section as a flat area with long tunnels behind, rising either side if the engine through the suspension. The clean nose shape he devised presented an air dam which divided the oncoming air stream into flows above and below the car. Underneath, the nose was designed to accelerate the air towards the tunnels. For Le Mans and Daytona Group 44 had a small single element wing that run without flaps. It was carried by subframe bolted to the back of the gearbox case, putting its loading directly into the chassis structure rather than the bodywork. Under GTP regulations the wing could extend no further back than the bodywork so Dykstra devised distinctive tail booms to carry the bodywork back as far as was necessary given his preferred wing and diffuser package. The tail swept gently downwards from the cockpit to well below the level of the wing and side fences led towards the short wing endplates.

The overall shape of the XJR-5 was extremely 'clean' with only small brake ducts in the nose, the radiators positioned centrally - flanking the firewall bulkhead - and fed through ducts in the vertical surfaces either side of the cockpit superstructure. Air was collected through the door and was exhausted over the rear wheel arch, through the tail section. Engine air was collected by a tail section top-duct position just behind the cockpit roof. There was only a single engine water cooler and this radiator was on the right. The other side was the oil radiator, behind which the engine bay carried a 20 litre oil tank (situated just ahead of the tyre).

The engine drove through a conventional AP $7^1/4$ inch racing clutch. This was a diaphragm spring unit with gear driven pressure plates. Sandwiched between the flywheel and the dished end cover carrying the diaphragm spring was a steel adapter ring with teeth cut into its inner surface. Those teeth meshed with teeth around the circumference of each steel pressure plate. The XJR-5 ran three pressure plates and the cover and adapter ring were bolted to a flywheel sized to match the outside diameter - 213mm. - of the adapter ring with a starter gear around it.

The steel flywheel and twin intermediate and main pressure plates worked in conjunction with steel driven plates onto which a bronze based friction material was sintered. The three driven plates were rigidly attached to hubs splined to the gearbox input shaft. Three plates were run for considerations of durability rather than torque. The input shaft ran under the differential into the outboard gearbox, Group 44 employing a conventional Hewland magnesium main case. However, it produced its own stronger sideplates for improved c.w.p. support.

The gearbox was a Hewland VG five speed. Brakes were conventional AP cast iron discs ventilated by internal radial slots. The disc was bolted to an alloy bell - saving weight - which was driven by the wheel drive pegs and was designed to function as an air pump, drawing air in from the brake ducting through the upright and flinging it out around its periphery. Four piston - 'four pot' - calipers were employed, one per disc bolted to the upright. The caliper was cast in aluminium as two halves which were bolted together with steel bolts. The pistons were aluminium and acted on Ferodo copper/asbestos pads.

The standard, 1.25 inch thick, 13" diameter disc brakes were buried within the wheel rims, which were of 16" diameter. Under GTP regulations both front and rear rims had to be of the same diameter. Group 44 fitted 11.5" wide fronts, 14" wide rears. These were of the modular type with a cast magnesium centre to which inner and outer aluminium alloy rims were bolted. The aluminium rims absorbed energy well in the event of impact and distorted rather than shattered or cracked should a driver hit a kerb on a street circuit. Group 44s modular wheels were at first supplied by Jongbloed but by '84 BBS was the supplier.

The brake discs and wheels were driven by six pegs and, as usual, the each wheel was retained by single nut. Tyres were, of course, supplied by Goodyear and were of traditional crossply construction. On board air jacks lifted the car clear of the ground in the event of a tyre change and for Le Mans car/pits communication was provided via a radio link.

The XJR-5 that Group 44 fielded at Le Mans in '84 was the product of an extensive weight saving campaign. The GTP minimum with a 6.0 litre two valve stock block engine was 900kg. and it had taken a lot of work including the development of lightweight Kevlar and carbon fibre composite body panels - to get close to this figure, the '82/'83 prototype having scaled something in the region of 975kg. Aerodynamics were subject to on going research by Dykstra who had undertaken hundreds of quarter scale model runs in various wind tunnels including the Williams Grand Prix team's rolling road facility. Rolling road model testing was the key to ground effect development but, as we have seen, the full sized car had also been checked for general aerodynamic configuration in the Lockheed fixed floor full size tunnel. A choice of underbody shapes had been developed to suit varying circuit characteristics: for Daytona and Le Mans there was less downforce and less drag, the two going hand in hand.

# Finishing the Job

The fact that Jaguar didn't succeed at its Le Mans comeback first or second time around was no disgrace for Group 44. Ford then Porsche had both made no-holes-barred attempts to overthrow the Le Mans establishment but each took three attempts to amass sufficient experience. However, as we have seen, a fundamental problem facing Group 44 at Le Mans was lack of Group C experience. Although the race offered a GTP category, all cars had to run to Group C fuel regulations. Crucially, Group 44 lacked the year round experience of running to a strictly limited quantity of regular octane fuel.

Jaguar's extremely professional European Touring Car Championship team Tom Walkinshaw Racing (TWR) had carefully built up the resources necessary to run a full Group C programme from its English base at Kidlington, near Oxford. And by the mid Eighties it had a track record that suggested that, given the right financial backing, it could win Group C races. Team boss Walkinshaw had started a Group C feasibility study in the summer of '84.

Group 44 had extracted impressive power from the Jaguar V12 engine running high octane fuel, only to flounder at Le Mans. Could a low octane Group C engine work? In Group C engine displacement was unlimited and sheer horsepower was not the challenge - fuel efficiency was. Could a two valve, normally aspirated engine hope to match the efficiency of a four valve turbo engine? Here the octane restriction was in the 'atmo' engine's favour - turbo engines had revolutionised Formula One only following the development of special fuels. In the turbo engine's favour was the flexibility afforded by the boost knob in the face of a fixed fuel allocation and changing race and weather conditions. And surely four valve engine technology was essential for race winning fuel efficiency?

Jaguar Engineering had a four valve development engine with chain driven d.o.h.c. heads. As Walkinshaw and Egan discussed the possibility of TWR moving into Group C this engine was dusted off and was slotted into the Jaguar XJR-5 chassis that had been displayed at the October '84 Motor Show, as previously recounted. TWR ran the car at Donington Park and Silverstone early in 1985. Nevertheless, TWR Engine Division manager Allan Scott was convinced he could make a Group C engine out of the two valve engine - a view many regarded with scepticism. Jaguar's V12 is not only heavy, it has an uncomfortable proportion of its weight high up and the experimental four valve heads were adding to that problem - to the tune of 30kg. Similarly, mild turbocharging was considered and rejected for the same reason of excess weight.

Engine performance is but part of the equation. The overall car package has to be right. Porsche had a highly developed, powerful and fuel efficient engine but a chassis that was somewhat dated by the standards of 1984. TWR could have continued with the XJR-5 chassis: the car was Group C legal and even conformed to the feet behind the front wheel axis ruling introduced for '85. The logistics of running an American built racing car were a problem, though. And TWR felt that the XJR-5 chassis was as dated as the Porsche with its aluminium monocoque base developed from a Seventies Can Am car. A brand new chassis could pay dividends.

Application of contemporary Formula One technology - in particular advanced composite materials technology for less weight yet greater rigidity - promised to help provide a clear chassis advantage. Further, the clean sheet of paper would allow the designer to aim at 850kg. - the IMSA minimum was 900kg. - and to optimise the weight distribution and to maximise the potential for ground effect aerodynamics as offered by Group C regulations.

The XJR-6 Group C car rolled out by TWR in '85 was a very different animal to the XJR-5, both in terms of chassis and engine. Although TWR was moving up from Group A racing its Group C engine was far from an evolution of its Group A engine. Scott had taken a clean sheet of paper and had devised a power plant featuring his own approach to combustion chamber design - it did not follow the Group 44 flathead development path and did not even share the same engine management system. Scott insisted on bringing the vital engine management system in house. Similarly the XJR-6 chassis owed nothing to Group 44 technology. Designed by Tony Southgate from a clean sheet of paper, it was a no compromise design to suit the Jaguar V12 engine and offered far more downforce than the Porsche 956/962 design with significantly greater rigidity.

In 1985 TWR got a feel for Group C with a short late season programme and early in '86 it won its first 1000km. race. Although too green to succeed at Le Mans, it should have won further 1000km. races that year - the XJR-6 had sufficient performance. However, having learned how to

*The XJR-6 arrived in 1985 : a new era had dawned*

fully dial the machine in to the various circuits TWR came back in devastating form in 1987, sweeping the World Championship. But Le Mans success remained elusive, in spite of the development of a bespoke Le Mans car with very special aerodynamics in view of the unique importance of drag over downforce at the French circuit.

Le Mans, as we have noted, requires experience and TWR was gaining that fast. It also requires strength in numbers. For 1988 TWR was able to expand from a three to a five car Le Mans effort by drawing upon its new IMSA team. The decision to switch the IMSA campaign from Group 44 to TWR was essentially political but looked logical in engineering terms. For a start, Group 44 had parted company with its car designer (in acrimonious circumstances) and when it came to the crunch TWR had developed a more advanced chassis and arguably a more effective race engine, though the fact that the IMSA engine lived on high octane fuel made direct comparison difficult.

Certainly, Scott's innovative move away from the flathead combustion chamber and his development of the engine management system in house, married to the application of advanced chassis technology and a clever approach to the weight distribution problem had paid dividends. The XJR-7 design employed some composite technology but was nowhere near as sophisticated as the Southgate design and Group 44 did not have a designer busy trying to remedy that.

Exploiting an adaptation of its Group C car, TWR started its IMSA campaign at the 1988 Daytona 24 hours, and won. It found less success at subsequent Camel GT races but won another World Championship *and* Le Mans with its 1988 Group C car, which was still an evolution of the '85 machine. The full story of the XJR-6/8/9's successful path to Le Mans is told on a year by year basis through the following four sections.

# Moving Up

If Jaguar had won the 1977 Silverstone TT the Broadspeed-run XJ12C ETCC programme might well have continued into 1978. Says driver/engineer Andy Rouse: "British Leyland could have had all the success it wanted in 1978. We needed time to develop away some of the problems of the car. If we had been able to do that, it would have won every race".

Success - for the first time - on home ground at Silverstone was the last chance a dismally unsuccessful two year project had of a reprieve. Rouse had spun off on oil chasing Tom Walkinshaw's leading BMW. Walkinshaw won.

Walkinshaw is a winner, as he proved time and again with foreign cars in the Seventies. He is also a patriot and he took the initiative to make ETCC winners out of British cars - the Rover 3500 and the Jaguar XJ-S - in the early Eighties. Without Walkinshaw a second Jaguar ETCC programme is unlikely to have happened. After the debacle of the XJ12C campaign Jaguar was far from looking for a way back into the series when Walkinshaw knocked on its door in 1980. But Walkinshaw had carefully studied the potential of the XJ-S in the light of new Group A regulations and he was able to win the confidence of John Egan.

Jaguar gave back door support and TWR's Group A project was planned from the outset to gather momentum at a careful pace. Publicity was deliberately kept low key until the results shouted for themselves. Walkinshaw's Kidlington based operation did a thoroughly professional job and soon had impressive results, winning races - including the Silverstone TT - as early as 1982. The team having proved itself, in 1983 Jaguar came out and gave the project open factory backing. More race wins followed in 1983 and '84, in which year Walkinshaw won the European title. "We were out there in British racing green", he recalls, "racing for Britain and proud of it. Jaguar was behind us fully, they weren't hiding any more and success obviously had a knock-on effect on the public, the workforce and the dealer networks around the world".

By this time, as we have seen, Jaguar had made a commitment to Le Mans. The return to the scene of its image-building Fifties success came together with privatisation of the company and, once started, was a job that clearly needed to be seen through to a successful conclusion. Le Mans is a formidable undertaking and it was thus somewhat inevitable that the highly professional, hugely successful and ambitious Jaguar racing team based in England should be drawn into the effort.

Le Mans '85 really highlighted the need for the TWR Group C project. After Tullius' finish faces were gloomy in the Group 44 encampment. Jaguar might have seen the chequered flag but it had never looked a threat, even with the fuel cut over '84. The talk was of lack of Group C experience, particularly in view of the engine detonation problem. If there were any doubts about the wisdom of the emerging TWR campaign they had been dispelled: Jaguar knew it could not win Le Mans with a GTP car.

Although TWR had already started its Group C project the XJR-6 could not be readied until after Le Mans '85. Successful racing cars are not born overnight. The ambitious project was managed by former Toleman Grand Prix Team Manager Roger Silman. Silman had first met Walkinshaw in the days when the Toleman Group's Formula Two team was run out of the TWR factory and he had kept in touch, "aware of Tom's ambitions". Silman had joined TWR early in '84 with no certainty of a Group C programme - but a likelihood of going to Le Mans with Jaguar had been an attractive alternative to Formula One.

Soon Silman was working on the Group C feasibility study. As he puts it: "the '84 Group A success led into Group C". In the early autumn he drew up a shortlist of three designers he felt capable of producing a state of the art machine to pitch against Porsche's "old fashioned" chassis. One of them was Tony Southgate.

Born in 1940, Southgate had served an engineering apprenticeship in his home town of Coventry while building 750 Formula racers as a hobby. That led to the youngster becoming Eric Broadley's first design assistant at Lola and he went on assist Ron Tauranac at Brabham. Having served Broadley and Tauranac Southgate joined Eagle in the late Sixties as the Californian concern's Chief Designer. In 1969 he went to BRM, then in the early Seventies to Shadow. Following a spell under contract to Lotus Southgate was part of the Shadow exodus that formed the Arrows team. He spent a few years as Technical Director at Arrows then, in 1980, he went freelance.

In September 1984 Southgate met with Silman, then with Walkinshaw. He shared their philosophy. This was Southgate's view as expressed to Racecar Engineering contributor Allan Staniforth: "The Porsche had been the car to beat for some time. It was quite obvious the chassis side was very basic, fairly flimsy construction, which

*Tony Southgate designed a chassis for the Cosworth-Ford turbo Group C car that threatened to relegate the Porsche 956 to the aerodynamic dustbin. Ford aborted the project for political reasons but TWR had spotted the potential...*

meant that the suspension side was not working as it should and the aerodynamics were very bitty. Stresses give the engine a hard time and crankcases start to break up. Porsche has the resources but is very slow to respond to racing needs..."

Southgate was given a simple brief: use the Jaguar V12 engine and apply Formula One technology. The problem for Southgate was that aerospace-developed composite materials had so far only been exploited by Formula One cars. A two metre wide advanced composite sportscar tub was a new departure in '84. Southgate had no doubts about the potential of the available materials and processes, but how to gain the necessary strength and rigidity from a significantly wider and more complex structure?

Southgate signed in October '84 to design a pioneering chassis that would be constructed and race engineered by TWR. Le Mans '85 was then the tentative target. Southgate would oversee car development while Silman managed the Group C operation. It was necessary for Silman to create an expanded, more ambitious race shop at Kidlington. Still based at his home studio, Southgate started work on November 1.

Aerodynamic form dominated Eighties racing car design and throughout November and December Southgate carried out extensive 20% model tests in the Imperial College rolling road wind tunnel (the facility John Barnard used during the McLaren MP4 design phase) and by Christmas he knew the general aerodynamic configuration. Thereafter, he worked at the drawing board while TWR continued to track test the four valve XJR-5 and to develop its own two valve engine, designed by Scott.

A Kiwi, Scott had raced and rallied at an amateur level and had run his own tuning business (renowned for extracting superb fuel economy from large displacement V8 engines) prior to emigrating to England in 1979. In England he found a job with the company that prepared Walkinshaw's Group A Mazda engine and that led to the offer to create TWR's own Engine Division.

With the Group A project there had been strong liaison between TWR and Jaguar Engineering and Jaguar Engineering had given Group 44 quite a lot of assistance, particularly in terms of the Lucas Micos system. Jaguar rather than Group 44 had commissioned Micos. TWR meanwhile had started working with ERA - Electronic Racing Aids - a small company formed by former Lucas employees Bill Gibson and Brian Mason. In the early Eighties Gibson and Mason had found Lucas slow to adapt to the emerging technology of engine management systems and had thus been spurred to branch out on their own.

In '84 ERA entered the limelight with a digital engine management system for the Hart Grand Prix engine. This was very similar to the Bosch Motronic system pioneered by the Porsche 956 and was a key factor in development of the Hart-

Toleman package to the extent that Senna was able to put it third on the grid for the '84 Estoril finale, just 0.4 second shy of pole.

For '85 Zytek Systems Ltd - as ERA now called itself - continued to develop its digital technology for Hart and looked to apply it to Scott's emerging Group C programme. With fuel efficiency the key factor engine management was going to play a central role. Scott was keen to keep the vital engine management system in house and this he could do with the support of Mason and Gibson's small, flexible concern. Indeed, from the engineering standpoint, TWR's Group C bid would be virtually autonomous. Jaguar's racing liaison manager Ron Elkins was subsequently transferred from Engineering to Sales and Marketing.

The XJR-6 build programme was able to commence in February '85, though detail parts drawing continued right up until June. TWR wanted to get race experience in '85, even if that meant rushing production of the prototype (which left Southgate and his assistant short of time for detail design work). Of course, throughout the build phase it had been clear that Le Mans was unrealistic. The car would not be race ready until July at the earliest.

Since through 1985 the TWR Group C race 'shop was under development, for logistical reasons the prototype car was constructed at the Wellingborough premises of TCP and ART. TCP - TC Prototypes Ltd - was the business run by master fabricator John Thompson. Thompson had started his career at McLaren in the mid Sixties then went to Cosworth to work on Robin Herd's 4-w-d car. Herd then invited him to participate in the formation of March but after a few years with the company he set up the TC Prototypes fabrication company and was soon producing aluminium monocoques for just about everyone in Formula One, from Amon to Williams. Even Ferrari ordered a Thompson monocoque in the mid Seventies. In the early Eighties Thompson built his own design Phoenix Indy Car and this was developed into the '82 Indy 500 winning Wildcat by the Patrick team.

ART - Auto Racing Technology Ltd - was a venture run jointly by Thompson and Southgate specialising in the production of race car bodywork. Together, TCP and ART could build a complete car, and Southgate could design it on behalf of the client. The partnership had already produced a Formula One car for Osella, the prematurely axed Ford Group C turbo car and the Ford RS200 rally car. Southgate and Thompson proposed doing all TWR's Group C car build but after the prototype phase TWR preferred to take assembly in house.

TWR sent staff to Wellingborough to participate in the prototype build and thereafter TCP and ART would continue fabrication work on behalf of TWR which concentrated on assembly. TCP did not have the facilities to produce the XJR-6's advanced composite tub in house so that was sub contracted from the outset to ACT - Advanced

Composite Technology Ltd - of Heanor, Derbyshire. Established in the Seventies by plastics in racing pioneer Roger Sloman, ACT had already produced carbon fibre and Kevlar based tubs for the likes of Euroracing and Ligier.

TWR had a contract to run Dunlop tyres - just as the works Porsche team - whereas Group 44 ran Goodyear. With its '84 privatisation Jaguar felt it should have an outside backer to help bear the inevitably huge cost of its projected Group C programme and since early '85 its Sales and Marketing department had been looking at possibilities. Castrol and Townsend Thorensen had made early commitments but only limited ones. To help land a big backer Jaguar turned early to Guy Edwards, motor racing's 'Mr Sponsorship'. Edwards produced the goods and in September '85 Jaguar and Gallaher, the tobacco giant, signed an agreement covering the three years 1986 - '88. A little later TWR agreed terms for those three seasons. In the meantime, it had launched its XJR-6 prototype.

Before studying the design of the new challenger, it is worth considering the state of Group C technology in the mid Eighties, prior to its arrival. Of particular interest are chassis construction and aerodynamics since in these areas TWR planned to score.

# GROUP C TECHNOLOGY

Born in 1982, Group C represented a fresh start for sportscar racing. The category essentially left engine choice free while restricting fuel via a maximum tank size of 100 litres and limits on the amount that could be consumed during a race. Fuel (of 102 octane maximum) was restricted to 510 litres for 1985 races of 1000km. duration. The minimum weight of a car was to be 850kg. and chassis regulations dictating a minimum windscreen height of 920mm. (within a maximum overall height of 1030mm.) ruled out 'spyder'-type cars.

Invariably, the Group C car was a fully enclosed coupe, often with a ground effect underbody. Maximum overall length was 4800mm. while maximum overall width was 2000mm. and the underbody sculpturing was restricted by the mandatory flat surface measuring at least 1000mm. wide and 800mm. long to be set within the wheelbase. Front and rear overhang were together not to exceed 80% of the wheelbase length while underbody sealing skirts were illegal.

Bodywork had to cover all the car's mechanicals and two doors (with windows for which a minimum size was specified) were mandatory. So was nominal passenger space in a cockpit of at least 1300mm. width: two seats and two footwells

had to be provided, disposed symmetrically either side of the car's centreline. The fuel tankage had to be accommodated within the wheelbase and within 650mm. either side of the car's centreline while the driver's feet had to be kept behind the front wheel axis from 1985 onwards. Of course, there were many, many prescriptions of a more detailed nature giving the Group C designer plenty to worry about.

In general terms, the XJR-5 was typical of the technology of the mid Eighties sports prototype on both sides of the Atlantic. However, it was only a matter of time before the advanced composite monocoque made its entrance. Advanced composite materials had been pioneered in Formula One since the early Eighties. The aims were to save weight and to add rigidity to the chassis structure, which in its entirety consists of the monocoque tub (housing driver, fuel tank and supporting the front suspension), the engine (plus attendant frame in the case of a semi-stressed engine) and the transaxle (invariably supporting the rear suspension).

It is important that the chassis structure is as rigid as possible, given high power and considerable downforce to cope with. Even with a low power car only fractional movement of one set of suspension pick up points relative to another will make a mockery of theoretical suspension performance. Lack of torsional rigidity will be perceived by the driver as unpredictable handling and will probably spoil a car's responsiveness to alterations intended to adjust its handling.

Excess weight is a serious handicap adversely affecting acceleration, braking, cornering performance, tyre wear and overall reliability. Informed opinion suggested every 10kg. excess weight added 0.2 - 0.3 seconds to a typical mid Eighties Formula One lap time. The need for a stiff yet slim and lightweight monocoque had seen Formula One 'wing car' designers turn from sheet aluminium tubs to aluminium honeycomb - a sandwich of thin inner and outer aluminium skins bonded to a core of paper thin honeycomb-form aluminium foil which acted as a continuous shear web, improving the strength:weight ratio.

While designers were starting to exploit the inherent stiffness of the aluminium honeycomb composite, moves were afoot that would lead to a switch to resin/fibre skins based on carbon or Kevlar sandwiching an aluminium foil or Nomex honeycomb core, again the core saving weight. The original resin/fibre material was glass reinforced plastic - g.r.p.- which set glass fibres in a polyester resin. The material was worked at atmospheric pressure and was cold rather than hot cured which made it easy to work. Strong it was not.

The breakthrough that paved the way for high performance plastic composites was hot cured epoxy resin which could be combined with fibres of glass, carbon or Kevlar. Glass was only a fraction of the price of the more advanced materials but had far less strength and much more weight. However, pressure bonded carbon and Kevlar based advance composite materials were more tear resistant than aluminium honeycomb, the product could be moulded to shape and the finished article had less weight and far greater torsional rigidity.

The strength of a resin/fibre composite is in the fibre. These materials incorporate fibres perhaps only 0.005" thick spun from glass, carbon or the DuPont Corporation's Kevlar aramid. While carbon and Kevlar fibres offer truly exceptional tensile strength and stiffness, they do so in only one direction: axially. Loads have to be fed along the axis of the fibres. The epoxy resin is used to envelope the fibres, after they have been woven into a cloth. The resin forms a plastic matrix which secures the fibres in the proper relationship to one another and bonds several layers together to a required thickness.

Weaves can be anything from a right angle lattice (50/50) to unidirectional and there is also the choice of fibre weight and stiffness for a given fibre type. The resin matrix offers no significant strength in its own right yet accounts for a high proportion of the total weight of a composite material. But it plays an indispensable role since, while it transmits loads to the fibres, it will not transmit cracks, and individual fibres can fracture without causing significant reduction in component strength as neighbouring fibres will consequently not be affected and will bridge the gap.

Generally an advanced resin/fibre composite is supplied as 'pre-preg' sheets which means that it is already impregnated with heat curing resin and only needs 'baking' under pressure once it has been worked into the shape of the component. This can be achieved by wrapping the unprocessed component in a vacuum bag and placing the bag in an oven or by using a special high pressure oven known as an autoclave, in which case higher pressures can be achieved.

Clearly there is an almost infinite choice of combinations of fibre, weave and resin that can be supplied as pre-preg material and thus it is produced to order. The key differences between carbon fibre and Kevlar are stiffness, impact resistance and cost. Carbon fibre is stiffer while Kevlar is less expensive and absorbs kinetic energy better. The combination of carbon fibre and Kevlar offers a good compromise between stiffness and impact resistance.

In 1981 McLaren International unveiled the first advanced composite monocoque car, the McLaren MP4 which employed carbon fibre skins. One week later Lotus unveiled the first carbon fibre/Kevlar car, and it was the latter combination that became the most widely employed in the early Eighties. However, McLaren bonded together five sections (including bulkheads) moulded to shape by American rocket maker Hercules, while Lotus formed its composite tub by folding up two panels to form a shell into which aluminium bulkheads

were inserted. Moulding to shape then bonding became the norm, the tub usually split into two main shell halves - either upper and lower or two sides - with bulkheads added, often of aluminium.

The crash resistance of composite tubs worried a number of designers while the technology was young. The traditional aluminium sheet monocoque deformed progressively and if properly designed would absorb a great deal of energy in the process. Advanced composites were acknowledged as stiff but it was feared that they would prove dangerously fragile upon secondary impact. A number of early Eighties tubs were designed with all or some of the outer skin aluminium though with greater experience of the materials this practice died out.

Experience of the materials themselves and of the possibilities associated with them saw Formula One designers achieve ever higher degrees of torsional rigidity. In 1962 Colin Chapman had pioneered the traditional aluminium monocoque registering a torsional rigidity in the region of 2500 lb. ft per degree. By the mid Eighties, with the use of advanced composites Formula One designers were able to achieve a figure comfortably in excess of 10,000 ft. lbs. per degree.

McLaren's trend setting MP4 design started the fashion not only for an advanced composite tub but also for the use of such materials as body panels, undertray, wings, brake ducts and so forth. For example, the radiators were carried in carbon fibre boxes strong enough to act both as mounts and ducting, replacing conventional metal subframes plus g.r.p. ducts. Ahead of the engine was less metal, less weight. The advanced composite monocoque Formula One car was stiff yet as light as the regulations permitted even when burdened with the weight of turbocharged engine ancillaries.

The advanced composite monocoque was a tempting if ambitious route for TWR as it set out to build an 850kg. car around a 250kg. engine and to exploit the full potential of underbody aerodynamics. The Porsche 956 was a ground effect car but arguably did not achieve the sort of downforce that was possible within the scope of Group C regulations. Group C car aerodynamics was a science that was still in its infancy in the mid Eighties.

Surprisingly, a ground effect racing car was first proposed in the September 1928 issue of *The Automobile Engineer*. Here correspondent R. Prevost, President of the Technical Committee of the Air Club of Algeria offered a concept for a Land Speed Record car chassis with the accompanying drawings and the following notes:

'Bearing in mind solely the side of the question concerned with aerodynamics, I had endeavoured to find a form of keel offering the minimum resistance to advance in the air while at the same time giving the machine the maximum stability and power of keeping on the track. In fact, I am convinced that by means of the rational study of

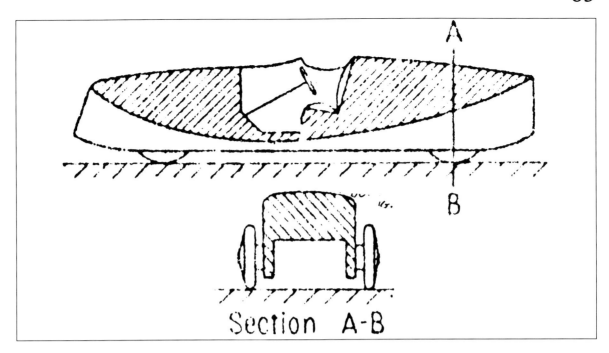

Section A-B

forms it would be possible with the tremendous speeds reached nowadays to utilise the flow of air around the keel, and also below it, to avoid the car's tendency to rise (to become 'unstuck' as we say in aviation).

'The keel in question resembles in outward shape though in rather rounded fashion, the silhouette of a rectangular parallelepiped. The underneath is nothing more than a Venturi tube, to be divided longitudinally by a plane, which in ideal circumstances should be the ground. In fact this division is made a little above the ground, for it is impossible not to leave a certain space, although as small as possible, between the ground and the lateral bows of the keel.

'In a word, I have endeavoured to allow the currents of air to flow with the minimum loss of pressure, while at the same time utilising the depression resulting from this flow to increase adhesion to the ground...'

Prevost had the right idea. The concept of an underbody venturi would go a long way.

Essentially, a venturi is a tube through which air (or fluid) passes, the cross section of which initially diminishes in area until it reaches a minimum, then increases again. The region where the area of cross section is at a minimum is called the throat. The shape of the cross section is immaterial and nor does it necessarily need to be the same along the length of the tube.

Air passing through the venturi tube accelerates as the tube converges, reaching maximum velocity at the throat, then decelerates again in the divergent part beyond, just as water flows faster where its channel is shallower. This form of acceleration is known as spatial acceleration since the change of velocity takes place in space as opposed to time - where velocity through a given space varies with time the acceleration is known as temporal. A venturi tube is designed to create a temporary spatial acceleration.

Bernoulli's Principle states that the higher the speed of a flowing fluid or gas, the lower its pressure - the venturi tube consequently creates a temporary pressure drop. Clearly the pressure will be lowest where the velocity is highest - in the throat.

Bernoulli's Principle similarly explains why an aircraft's wing creates lift: the wing is shaped so that air flowing over it has a longer, faster route than that passing underneath. Air flowing over a traditional car shape has a longer route than that flowing underneath, creating an unwanted tendency for the car to lift. This problem becomes more acute as speed increases - hence Prevost's concern for the stability of the Land Speed Record cars of the Twenties.

Of course, an inverted aircraft wing can be mounted above a car to generate negative lift - downforce - and Prevost may well have thought of that. The important point, as Prevost makes clear, is that, in theory, his underbody venturi has little adverse effect in terms of the resistance caused by the vehicle to the on coming air.

Clearly, molecules of air have to be pushed aside for a vehicle to pass through it and the amount of energy required to push the molecules apart is affected by the vehicle's shape and represents its drag. Further, there is 'shape drag' and 'downforce drag'. Downforce is always won at a cost measured in terms of increase of drag. The generation of any form of lift - negative or positive - requires energy and that saps the energy available to overcome air resistance, while drag can be seen as the horizontal component of lift which is never purely vertical in effect. However, different aerodynamic devices cause different amounts of drag for a given amount of downforce. Prevost's was a low drag solution.

Aircraft employ wings with a slotted flap at the back which increases lift at a significant cost in terms of drag. However, once the aircraft has taken off the flap can be retracted. Racing cars need a wing with a slotted flap - the dual element wing - to create substantial downforce for improved cornering but regulations invariably ban the retraction of the flap on the straightaway.

An alternative method of pressure reduction is to seal the front and sides of the vehicle while leaving the rear open - the so called 'open tailed box' method. If an efficient method of sealing can be devised a partial vacuum will be created, though the tendency for high pressure air to migrate in through the tail opening spoils the efficiency of this approach. However, if the rear is also sealed off and a powered fan is used to extract air the result will be dramatic. This was demonstrated by Chaparral's late Sixties 2J Can Am 'fan car' which represented a quantum leap in cornering potential. The concept was quickly banned by motor racing authorities throughout the world.

Chaparral also experimented with a pure venturi tube car as anticipated by Prevost but this did not work since the on coming air caused sufficient build up of pressure at the high venturi inlet to make the front wheels go light. Nevertheless, the basic principle of venturi-type underbody airflow acceleration could be adapted to achieve impressive results as Lotus demonstrated in the late Seventies with its revolutionary Formula One 'wing car' car.

The confusingly-named 'wing car' moved underbody aerodynamics out of the realm of pure venturi theory as applied, for example, to obtain a pressure drop to mix air and fuel in a carburettor. It recognised that a racing vehicle is passing at high speed through essentially stationary air, that its underbody runs in very close proximity to the ground and that the desired pressure reduction is not at one specific point but is over as much of the underbody as possible.

Lotus showed how, through careful underbody design it is possible to achieve highly beneficial spatial acceleration of air beneath a racing car. The magnitude of the pressure drop it is possible to obtain relates to the path provided for the air and to the speed of the vehicle: aerodynamic forces generally increase with the square of velocity. Further, the planform area over which the underbody pressure reduction acts has to be considered.

*Wind tunnel model of Porsche 956 reveals the car's underwing.*

Atmospheric pressure pushes down on a car at 14.7p.s.i. at sea level (less as altitude rises and the air thins). If pressure is reduced underneath, the car will be pressed towards the track by a force equal to the mean pressure differential multiplied by the planform area in question. A sports prototype has a planform area in the region of 14,000 square inches: if, at a given speed, there is a mean pressure differential over the planform of only 0.15p.s.i. the product is 2100 pounds of downforce - more than the car's own weight (typically a sports-prototype is in the region of 1900/2000lb.).

Whereas a conventional car tends towards lift, a racing car with wings to create downforce and a flat bottom run at very low ground clearance (for a low centre of gravity) tends towards low pressure in the underbody region. That is a start. In the mid Seventies Gordon Murray achieved useful downforce through fitting a vee-shaped, snowplough like skirt under the belly of his winged, flat bottom Brabham Grand Prix car. Air was deflected away from the area behind the skirt, where a partial vacuum formed.

Lotus went further setting a long shallow venturi-style throat under each sidepod with a small, carefully contoured funnel-type inlet leading into it (this was situated close behind the front wheel) and a carefully contoured 'diffuser' section behind it, rising alongside the drivetrain. A diffuser is simply a device designed to convert a high velocity low pressure airstream into a low velocity high pressure flow. In this case it returned air speeded up through the throat to its natural velocity, avoiding a net loss of efficiency. The diffuser acted both to provide properly controlled deceleration of the airflow - essential for proper working of the ground effect underbody - and to draw air through the throat.

More air speeded up means more low pressure air while the flow has to be speeded up as much as possible and to be held at high speed for as long as possible to create the maximum downforce. A danger is of a high pressure build up at the entrance to the throat which migrates back, wiping out low pressure. Similarly, uncontrolled air in the diffuser costs potential downforce and saps energy, increasing drag.

Hereafter we shall refer to an entire ground effect underbody form as an 'underwing'. The operation of the underwing is clearly influenced by the overall body shape. However, it is worth stressing that an underwing works on the principle of the venturi rather than as a form of inverted aircraft wing.

Considering the overall shape of the body, the nose profile influences how air enters the underwing while the tail form influences its extraction - and if positioned properly a rear wing can be a very powerful force, its local effect pulling air through the tunnels. Ideally an underwing will be flanked laterally by sliding skirts bridging the gap between the bodywork and the track surface.

These stop air migrating from the sides of the car to the low pressure area underneath, a phenomenon which clearly reduces the pressure drop.

With or without skirts, the operation of the underwing should be relatively insensitive to pitch since this varies as a car proceeds around a track. The location of the centre of pressure tends to move with pitch changes.

The downforce generated will not be so much use if the aerodynamic balance is all wrong. An aerodynamic split 30:70 front:rear is about the best that can be achieved, and it is important that the centre of pressure stays near enough where the designer intends it should be. Ground effect cars tend to run raked with the front lower than the rear and compromised around the ideal angle of attack. A sports-prototype requires higher ground clearance than a single seater due to its wider monocoque and with its larger planform area will tend to be more pitch sensitive.

The infamous Formula One 'wing cars' of the late Seventies and early Eighties initially ran sliding skirts though these were subsequently outlawed. The skirted underwings were extremely effective and front and rear wings were asked to produce very little downforce in their own right, acting virtually as trim tabs, since underbody downforce is won at a lower drag penalty. Partly through cleaning up the underbody flow. Indeed, as underwing performance improved front wings started to fade away altogether.

Although '83 'flat bottom' Formula One regulations called for the entire expanse of underbody between the front and rear wheels to be a uniformly flat surface, it was possible, in effect, to treat this as an area through which air could be gainfully accelerated by carefully controlling the flow to the region and by setting a diffuser behind the mandatory flat area. In its simplest form, the 'diffuser' was merely a short upsweep at the end of the flat bottom area. The upsweep had to be split either side of the gearbox but if so desired could be extended as far as the maximum permissible 600mm. rear overhang (measured from the rear wheel axis).

Each of the flat bottom Formula One car's twin diffuser upsweeps provided a focus for the general influx of air characteristic of an unsealed underbody region. If the underwing worked properly, air accelerated as it squeezed under the nose and sidepod floor; got another 'kick' as it squeezed between the rear wheels; yet another as it funnelled into a diffuser entrance - the venturi throat.

Acceleration of air into the upsweeps caused the biggest pressure drop, and there was the important choice of short 'flip up' or long diffuser ramp. In the case of the former, the area under the rear deck worked like an open tailed box scavenged by the local effect of the rear wing and created a partial vacuum, helping draw air through the upsweep. In the case of the latter, the extended ramps drew in air, again assisted by the wing and generally assisted by the action of the exhaust, a principle introduced by Renault during the '83 season.

With exhaust blown diffuser ramps, a pipe was led into the base of each ramp so that the gas flow would help 'activate' the airflow on the underside. It should be noted that a full length diffuser ramp was active on both sides for airflow through the engine bay would create useful pressure on its pronounced upswept upper surface. However, the overall package was very subtle: in each case there was a complex interaction between the underwing, the tail shrouding and the rear wing. An extended, exhaust blown diffuser worked well with a pronounced 'bottleneck' plan rear end, as in the case of the McLaren MP4, while a 'flip up' worked well with a relatively high and wide tail shroud, as in the case of the 1983 title winning Brabham BT52. Brabham could not get an extended diffuser to work without exhaust activation, and had only one exhaust pipe to play with.

While it was possible to decrease the inherently low pressure under a flat bottom car, the front and rear wings now had to supply well over half of the total downforce: a return to large front wings was indicative of the renewed importance of conventional wings for a flat bottom mid Eighties Formula One car. However, there was more potential for underwing performance in Group C, though the flat area ruling caused a problem for entrants wishing to use the ground effect March 83/85C, a car designed to IMSA GTP regulations. The March employed Formula One wing car style tunnels either side of its monocoque floor, which was less than 1000mm. wide.

The dominant Group C car of 1983/'84 was, of course, the Porsche 956. The Porsche incorporated the mandatory flat area within a full length, recessed central underwing (this reminiscent of Prevost's original venturi car design, though with a much lower inlet). The nose was free of a radiator and had a low central notch fashioned so as to funnel air to the flat area. Behind the mandatory flat area, the car's short, wide flat six engine and its transaxle titled upwards to make room for a wide, gentle central diffuser upsweep interrupted only by the relatively narrow 'blister' needed at the back to clear the gearbox. However, since the engine had air cooled cylinders it was necessary to set ventilation slots into the forward section of the diffuser. Arguably worse, the 956 had been designed without reference to rolling road wind tunnel tests.

To properly explore underbody aerodynamics it is necessary to employ a moving ground plane, or 'rolling road' wind tunnel since the relationship between a moving vehicle and the stationary ground is an important influence upon the underbody airflow, primarily due to so called shear forces. If both the vehicle and the ground are stationary an artificial 'boundary layer' is formed. Traditional wind tunnel testing is not conducive to effective underwing design. Nevertheless, the Porsche 956 was a highly successful racing car... in the absence of powerful opposition.

Principal rival Lancia likewise relied upon traditional fixed floor wind tunnel model testing. When in 1983 Tony Southgate was employed by Ford to design the turbo Ford Group C car he went to work with 20% models in the Imperial College, London rolling road tunnel. Southgate devised an underwing headed by a splitter and with 'wing car' type tunnels channelled either side of the flat bottom area. In fact, behind the mandatory flat area were twin, two level tunnels leading into the generous diffusers that rose either side of the Cosworth/Hewland (Formula One-type) drivetrain. As wide as possible, the diffuser upsweeps took the usual, unavoidable S-shaped route between the narrowing drivetrain and the rear wheels. Southgate confirmed that airspeed lost in the first part of the 'S' was regained in the second part, cancelling out any negative effect.

Unlike Porsche and Lancia, Southgate set his rear wing remote from the rear deck since, as in the case of Formula One wing cars, the wing was used primarily to help extract air from the diffuser tunnels which exited underneath it. A small rear wing was employed which created 300lb. of downforce in its own right but which by its positioning created an extra 600lb. of downforce under the car. Wind tunnel research confirmed that the wing's local air flow helped pull air through the underwing and this in turn allowed the use of steeper diffuser tunnels. A smooth rear deck was essential to be able to use the rear wing this effectively.

For a Formula One car the rear body was a nuisance, spoiling the flow to the rear wing. For a sports-prototype it could be put to good effect, delaying drag inducing separation of the so called 'laminer' flow over the body and putting the rear wing to work in cleaner air. Of course, with its enclosed wheels and all enveloping body the sports-prototype generated far less drag than the Formula One car. Indeed, a good proportion of the drag of a Formula One car is caused by its rotating exposed wheels.

Various devices have long been employed to manipulate the aerodynamics of the traditional coupe bodied sports-prototype, including concave nose panels and front wheel arch louvers, both to add downforce. Louvers bleed air off, equalising pressure above and within the arch: this reduces pressure within, at the usual penalty of increased drag. A nose splitter will also add downforce and drag.

Although downforce is generally the primary concern, drag is a factor that cannot be ignored. As we have seen, high downforce invariably implies a high drag penalty and this becomes of more concern given Group C's emphasis upon fuel efficiency. Fuel efficiency is a function of engine performance, car weight and car drag. As we have noted, drag is of two types: downforce drag and shape drag. Shape drag is a product of frontal area, a non dimensional air drag co-efficient - the Cd (Cw in Germany, Cx in France) - and velocity. And while the drag force increases with the square of velocity, in theory the horsepower spent overcoming it increases with the cube of velocity.

Aerodynamicists tell us that it is easier to 'pull' than to 'push' air and thus, in aerodynamic terms, the front of a sports-prototype is effectively blunt while the rear shape does the work in reducing drag. The cockpit is situated well forward and, in trying to compress, the on coming air tends naturally to follow the lines of the nose and windscreen. Behind the cockpit the natural tendency is for the air to separate from the body causing drag. The right shape pulling the air will delay separation.

The lowest drag shape is that of a tear drop. At the other end of the spectrum is a parachute. A parachute has a Cd of 1.35, while a flat plate has one of 1.17. A hemisphere has a Cd of 0.41 while a sphere is lower still at 0.10. Typically, a road car will measure in the region of 0.40 but Ford's Probe IV design study recorded 0.137 - less than a McDonnell Douglas F-15 fighter.

If a hemisphere faces the oncoming air a partial vacuum forms behind it (at the flat back surface) since less air passes there than over its domed face. This causes drag. It is avoided by guiding the air behind the curved face of the hemisphere: hence a lower drag co-efficient for the teardrop form. In the case of the sports prototype, a carefully shaped dorsum keeps the air flow attached - hence the sloping tail profile of the traditional whale shaped coupe, as typified by the original Porsche 917.

However, as Porsche discovered with its first powerful coupe, streamlining is less important than downforce on a conventional road course. Very low drag is at the cost of high speed stability and, of course, implies low downforce. To make it driveable, the Porsche 917 needed to abandon its classical downward sloping, low drag tail for a high rear deck design that added downforce while increasing its Cd from 0.4 to 0.447. The switch followed tests at the Osterreichring circuit. The car's creator Doctor Ferdinand Piech told the author: "all Porsche coupes up to the Osterreichring had a tail with a rounded rear part. In the wind tunnel the aerodynamics were much better. But previous cars had too little power, with the 917 suddenly we had too much. Aerodynamic stability was suddenly a very important factor. We saw from this modification that this did help much more. Reducing top speed and gaining stability was the right way to go".

Although the higher drag of the revised 917 cost top speed, the cornering advantage it bestowed at the Osterreichring was such that Porsche racing car designer Hans Mezger compared it to a 50 b.h.p. increase in engine power. Since downforce tends thus to be more significant than drag, the mid Eighties Group C car designer was less concerned with the drag factor than with the lift to drag ratio.

In general, it is possible to achieve a higher lift:drag ratio with a high downforce ground effect car. A figure of 3:1 was very good for a mid Eighties sports-prototype. Designers were reluctant to reveal actual figures, though Ray Mallock says he managed to improve the "less than one" ratio for the original flat bottom Aston Martin-Nimrod to "2:1" through careful massaging of the shape without having the possibility of resorting to an underwing. Southgate's ground effect Group C Ford was said to produce a maximum of 4000lb. downforce - twice its own weight - for a cost of 1200lb. drag, giving it a ratio of 3.3:1. That illustrates the greater efficiency of an effective ground effect underbody over wings.

Le Mans is the only circuit where drag is the overriding consideration. This, of course, is due to the three and a half mile long Mulsanne straight, where speeds in excess of 220 m.p.h. are commonplace, as against a maximum of 180 m.p.h. elsewhere. Since downforce increases with the square of velocity it can increase alarmingly on the Mulsanne - where it is unwanted and brings the danger of excessive component stress, perhaps including overheated tyres. On the other hand lower downforce, lower drag and higher speed on the Mulsanne can pay dividends. Often there is a choice between this option or lower Mulsanne speed and higher cornering speed to achieve a given lap time. The lower downforce option has the advantage that it helps the driver pass in the easiest place - on the straight - and, more significantly, it will be the lightest on fuel.

The classic solution for Le Mans is a long tail, designed to discourage air separation for as long as possible. The long tail has, however, the disadvantage that it can reduce drag to the extent that instability becomes dangerous. Further, it can make a car somewhat unwieldy. Derek Bell described the classic Porsche 917 Langheck as "like having a caravan on the back!" A further disadvantage of the traditional long tail is that it cannot be used effectively in conjunction with a ground effect underbody.

A low drag ground effect Le Mans car potentially has the best fuel efficiency and is unlikely to suffer a dangerous loss of downforce but if the centre of pressure is in the wrong place - in other words too far forward - the car may be difficult to control. And the emphasis is on low drag, as early ground effect Group C cars discovered. High downforce on the Mulsanne is not only unwanted - as we have suggested, it can be a liability.

Regardless of underbody aerodynamics, a single element rear wing is generally appropriate for Le Mans. It might be less efficient as a means of creating high downforce but at this circuit it tends to offer the right downforce/drag compromise. Endplate size also tends to shrink, to the same effect. Endplates play a significant role in the operation of a racing car wing - a fact that highlights the subtlety of the science of sports-prototype aerodynamics. A science that TWR aimed to push forward.

# Fresh Approach

## TWR Group C V12

60 degree V12

92.0 x 78.0mm./ 6219.0cc
Unblown
Aluminium block and heads
Wet cast iron liners
7 main bearings, plain
Steel crankshaft, 6 pins
Steel con rods
Cosworth light alloy pistons
Goetze rings
S.o.h.c., chain driven
2 valves/cylinder, 1 plug
Parallel valves
50mm. inlet valve, 41mm. exhaust
Lucas ignition
Bosch injection
Zytek engine management system
Compression ratio 12.0:1
Maximum r.p.m. 7,600
250kg. including clutch

As we have seen, TWR started its long involvement with Jaguar racing a Group A XJ-S. Group A imposed restrictions on inlet valve size and valve lift and the original exhaust manifold had to be retained, though pistons, camshafts and other engine internals were free. The 1982 debuted TWR XJ-S was fuel injected as per the standard car and a wet sump was retained, as demanded by the regulations, with complex baffling to keep the oil under control.

The ultimate Group A engine had been achieved by the time of the 1984 season following porting and camshaft work, and the introduction of revised pistons which were run with a slightly higher compression ratio. The production injection had given way, first (in '83) to an ERA supplied analogue electronic injection system, then to a digital system and 450 b.h.p./ 7,300 r.p.m. had been attained within the strict breathing restrictions.

For Group C, Scott, unhindered by mandatory engine specifications, could make a fresh start. He knew the two valve V12 well and (unlike some of his colleagues) felt sure it could form the basis of a competitive Group C engine, even though a four valve engine should inherently be more fuel efficient. As we have seen, the four valve option did not appear favourable in the light of chassis considerations. In place of Jaguar's top heavy four valve development engine, Scott offered his own thinking on combustion chamber design.

Clearly, Scott was free to develop the classic flathead combustion chamber design as Group 44 had done, or alternatively a flat piston crown design - not necessarily along the lines of the May Fireball chamber - or to devise a chamber partially in the piston, partially in the head. He understandably would not divulge his design, which was the key to the performance of the TWR Group C engine. It was not a straightforward development of his earlier Group A engine and it did not follow the Group 44 path. Indeed, there was no input from the Group 44 engine programme. Scott went his own way on the basis of what he had learned in Group A plus his own, fresh ideas (and, as we have noted, he continued to work with Zytek (nee ERA) engine management rather than use the factory commissioned Micos system).

Having convinced TWR to stay with the two valve single cam 'Hassan' head, Scott is is unreserved in his praise for its porting. He says it flows extremely well: "somewhere between the

best of any other two valve and a four valve head". Its semi-downdraught inlet port design (with only a gentle S-bend between overhead inlet manifold flange and valve seat) must take much credit for this and Scott says he was able to develop a Group C engine offering 100% volumetric efficiency over the maximum torque period. The major drawbacks of any two valve head are the location of the spark plug (unavoidably offset) and less valve area than it is possible to attain given four valves in the same area. To get more valve area Scott went for a bigger bore.

Whereas Group 44 was confined to a 6.0 litre displacement in '85, Scott went for a same (78mm.) stroke crankshaft (this TWR employed in an XJ-S road conversion) but for a bigger (92mm. rather than the traditional 90mm.) bore to achieve a displacement of 6.2 litres.

The prototype TWR Group C engine ran an 11.8:1 compression ratio (compared to 11.5:1 for the Group A engine) and offered 640b.h.p. By the time the TWR campaign commenced Scott's Zytek managed engine was running a 12.0:1 compression ratio - in spite of the relatively low (maximum 102) octane Group C fuel - and offered 650/660b.h.p. at 7,000r.p.m. As we have seen, in '85 Group 44 claimed a similar output at slightly higher r.p.m. and from a slightly smaller capacity: a reflection of its far higher octane fuel.

Of course, the GTP car did not have to pay the same attention to fuel consumption. At first, in '85, the XJR-6 was overweight and with an eye to the fuel allowance Scott set the race r.p.m. limit at 6,500r.p.m. However, with development weight would come down and Scott knew he would then be able to run more power from even larger displacements. Porsche had gone from from 650b.h.p. in '83/4 (when the TWR engine evolved) to 700b.h.p., primarily through the switch from mechanical to fully electronic injection.

Often electronic engine technology had caused headaches in terms of 'noise' interference: a microprocessor's sophisticated circuits are highly sensitive to interference in the form of electro-magnetic pulses generated mainly by the ignition system. This calls for very careful location and insulation of the ECU (electronic control unit) and its wiring. Scott anticipated potential noise problems and cleverly avoided them right from the outset of the Group C programme.

Scott's Group C engine was based on a remachined production block, modified externally for chassis installation purposes and internally to accept bigger bore liners. Steel four bolt main bearing caps replaced the cast iron production items while TWR fitted a magnesium dry sump pan as a stiffening structure, albeit retaining the stock sump fixing points.

As with the block, Engine Division worked from Jaguar supplied aluminium head castings, the heads having a separate tappet block which was closed via a TWR produced magnesium cam cover. Again production fixings were retained, each head

thus attached via 26 studs: each cylinder was surrounded by a six bolt pattern with adjacent cylinders sharing a pair of studs. TWR additionally doweled the heads to the block to avoid any danger of shifting - important since the engine was run as a heavily stressed chassis member.

Although the V12 was long and heavy it was sufficiently robust to accept the major proportion of the chassis load: it was bolted firmly to the rear bulkhead and in turn the transaxle was primarily bolted to it. However, there was a single tube each side linking the rear bulkhead directly to the bellhousing to add a little to rigidity in the horizontal plane. The rear bulkhead was attached to the front of the sump and the cam covers and additional stays ran from the integral cockpit roll hoop to a point midway along each cam cover.

As we have seen, the deep monobloc, wet iron liner V12 paid for its rugged construction with a total weight of 250kg. Scott ran cast iron liners located as per standard, via a flange situated just over 44mm. down the depth of the bore which left the hottest part of the liner in direct contact with the coolant. Flange sealing employed a sealing compound, a troublefree solution. Sealing at the deck employed sealing rings and a perimeter gasket, the detail design of which was a closely guarded secret, one that Group 44 did not share...

The crankshaft was another TWR development. It was very similar in design to the production item but was significantly lighter. It was a special nitrided EN40B steel forging produced using TWR's own tooling. Since the 60 degree V12 engine was inherently balanced Scott was able to save the weight of a vibration damper. The flywheel was attached via ten bolts and was sized to match a regular 71/4 inch clutch, while carrying a starter ring. For reasons of chassis installation the starter motor was mounted at the front of the engine, turning a long shaft.

The TWR crankshaft ran standard diameter main bearing journals but smaller (2.1" rather than 2.3") diameter con rod journals. Vandervell supplied the plain bearings while H-section forged EN24 steel con rods were machined outside to TWR requirements. The rod length retained the production 6" from centre to centre and the cap was attached via two capscrews. The bushed small end carried a fully floating steel gudgeon pin retained by conventional circlips.

As usual, three Goetze rings were carried above the gudgeon pin. The piston was a Cosworth forging to a TWR design (apparently evolved from the Group A programme) and was cooled via an oil spray. The piston design was one of the factors allowing a high compression ratio to be run in spite of poor quality fuel. The head retained a production plug location and TWR achieved excellent results from its flow work thanks to the aforementioned excellence of the stock port design.

The valve seats and guides were bronze based while the vertical valves were solid stainless steel, the precise material specifications very carefully chosen. Dual Schmitthelm springs and steel bucket tappets were fitted. The steel camshaft was lighter than standard, was machined from solid and heat treated. It ran directly in the head, retained, production-style, by aluminium caps. The camshaft drive sprocket was connected via the Jaguar production system which offered timing adjustment via fine internal and external teeth.

The drive from the front of the crank naturally retained the production take off point between the first main bearing and the front cover and employed a lightweight steel sprocket. As with the production engine, a single two-row Duplex roller chain was used, this fitted with a TWR modified tensioner. As usual ,the chain passed around the crankshaft sprocket, the two camshaft sprockets and the regular jackshaft sprocket, TWR retaining the production distributor drive. The jackshaft ran down the central valley to a mid point where bevel gears drove an upright Lucas distributor.

The water and oil pumps were driven from a toothed pulley on the nose of the crankshaft, the bank of oil pumps positioned low down alongside the block while (as standard) the water pump was in the centre of the front cover. The alternator was positioned on the other side, higher up and was driven via a vee-belt from the water pump. The oil pumps were in sandwich - one pressure and four scavenge for the long crankcase. Oil pressure was 50p.s.i., restricted to 10p.s.i. for the camshafts.

Exhaust tuning was of major importance. TWR employed a three into one then two into one system system for each bank whereas Group 44 had tended to favour further blending into a single tail pipe. Scott established a fixed length of inlet trumpet applicable to all circuits, the trumpets fixed to a throttle slide bank sitting atop short individual inlet tracts. The injectors (one per cylinder) were positioned in the trumpets just above the slides.

TWR's Zytek engine management system controlled Bosch supplied solenoid injectors and a Lucas CD ignition system which fired a single 14mm. Champion plug per cylinder. There was a back up crankshaft trigger. Developed from the Group A programme, the Zytek system was housed in a single box. The major development for Group C was a switch from Group A-type non-sequential to more precise, fully computer timed sequential injection. The key ECU inputs were speed and throttle angle and Scott was cagey about other readings. However, it was no secret that TWR had a driver-adjustable mixture control, according to the setting of which the ignition curve was programmed. Engine Division did its own software development with support from Zytek and mapping was a continual process at its well equipped Kidlington 'shop. A regular engine strip down and rebuild was reckoned to occupy 100 hours, including a final dyno check.

# Art and Science

## TWR XJR-6

Advanced Composite Technology carbon fibre/
Kevlar monocoque
Stressed engine
Push rod front, conventional rear suspension
Koni and Bilstein dampers
Speedline magnesium rims
AP cast iron discs, outboard
Single AP four pot calipers, Ferodo pads
Carbon fibre/Kevlar bodywork
1 Serck water radiator
1 Behr oil: water heat exchanger
AP triple plate clutch
March five speed gearbox - Salisbury diff
100 litre fuel tank, 19 litre oil tank
Varley battery - Smiths instruments
2780mm. wheelbase; 1550mm. front track,
1500mm. rear.
900kg.

"It was obvious that the engine would dominate the car in terms of performance, due to its weight, the position of its centre of gravity and its length", says Southgate. " The position of the fuel was less important than the position of the engine, so the engine was put as close as possible to the driver".

The possibility of moulding complex shapes from advanced composite materials enabled Southgate to design a monocoque that cleverly optimised the difficult packaging this implied. Basically, he slotted the front of the engine through the front engine bay wall into space behind the driver's seat that would otherwise have been occupied by the fuel tank. The tank compartment was then moulded around the engine inset, both flanking it and extending forwards to form the sloping back of the seat.

The unconventional recess in the back of the monocoque which accommodated the front portion of the engine was 100mm. deep. By overlapping the engine and monocoque to this extent Southgate was able to keep the long engine far enough from the rear wheel axis to promote good weight distribution, given the requirement to keep the driver's feet behind the front wheel axis together with wheelbase constraints.

The chosen wheelbase dimension of 2780mm. was a response to aerodynamic requirements, heavily compromised by the regulations (and further influenced by the special demands of the V12 package). For Group C eligibility it was necessary to keep front plus rear overhangs to within 80% of the wheelbase dimension while keeping to an overall maximum length of 4800mm. For aerodynamic reasons Southgate wanted generous rear wing and nose overhang and plenty of planform area.

Within the basic package, weight distribution was further influenced by a choice of front location for the engine radiator and by siting the oil tank at the front of the engine bay rather than in the bellhousing contemporary Formula One style. The novel engine location plus these measures helped Southgate achieve a conventional 40 - 60 front - rear distribution in spite of the unusual length and weight of the V12. It was also necessary for him to counter the high centre of gravity of the V12 as far as possible. With a dry sump and a flywheel matching a 7 1/4 inch racing clutch the engine had been designed to mount low and Southgate aimed to mount all chassis components as low as possible, and to keep the fuel load as low as he could.

Aside from the location of major components

with a view to good weight distribution, aerodynamic considerations dictated Southgate's XJR-6 design. As we have seen, tunnel testing of 20% models dominated the early design phase. Southgate worked towards a 'sprint' package - a Le Mans version would follow later. He had done a lot of wind tunnel work for the Ford Group C project and admits that this benefited the new design. However, the XJR-6 did not share the same type of underwing. Rather than recessing venturi sections into the floor of the monocoque Southgate used the entire expanse of the car's belly to prepare the air for its rush into the engine bay diffuser tunnels.

Intriguingly, Southgate says he started out with twin front radiators before adopting a more conventional nose layout. A splitter formed the leading edge of the underwing and the complexity of ground effect aerodynamics can be judged from the fact that this was just one of eight items at the front of the car influencing downforce. Underneath, horizontal wheel sealing plates were fitted to extend the underwing plan area as close as possible to the front wheels (leaving just enough room for steering movement) while at the sides of the car, running back from the front wheel arches were horizontal skirts which echoed the ledges formed ahead of the arches by the flanks of the splitter.

Keeping the monocoque to 100mm. less than the maximum 2000mm. overall width (which, for example, was fully utilised by the Porsche 956 tub) offered a reduced frontal area and allowed prominent skirts to be fitted. The skirts were carried as far back as possible and played an important role in the operation of the underwing, confusing air rushing down the car's flanks and thus discouraging flow to the underbody.

Ahead of the engine bay diffuser tunnels, the planform area was flat. The diffuser tunnels commenced immediately behind the monocoque and rose steeply either side of the drivetrain. As with the Ford, the tunnels were designed to work in conjunction with a remote, dual element rear wing which was mounted on a central gearbox post above the exit from the underwing.

The general body shape was designed primarily to benefit the operation of the underwing and the rear wing. With the nose radiator only one major air inlet was required, logically set over the splitter. The inlet was formed in a forward panel that concealed the near horizontal radiator. This panel was carefully contoured, concave to add downforce and blended into the front wheel arches which were louvered on top to add further downforce. Hot radiator air exhausted behind the short concave panel, across a sloping scuttle that blended into the windscreen.

The windscreen was as low and narrow as was permitted and its dimensions defined the maximum cross sectional area of the central superstructure. Behind the cockpit, a streamlined dorsum blended into a flat rear deck which was flanked by rear wheel arch bulges. The rear bodywork was designed to feed air smoothly to the rear wing. The wing was set higher than the deck, to which no rear spoiler was fitted. Only the leading edge of the two piece (main element plus slotted flap) wing overlapped the deck: there was a critical spatial relationship between the deck and the wing.

Underneath, the tunnels ran as far as the rear deck and rose almost to its height. As we have noted, the underwing incorporated the entire monocoque floor area as a flat surface (within which was the mandatory flat area). Forming wide venturi throats, the tunnel entrances measured much of the span of the rear bulkhead either side of the engine recess. The inner tunnel walls hugged the drivetrain while the outer walls curved inwards to clear the rear wheels. Although the tunnel plan narrowed, the growth in height was made to compensate: the three dimensional form of the tunnels was all important and this increased evenly in terms of cross sectional area.

Careful suspension design kept the tunnels free of all but the driveshafts and lower wishbone arms and thus both relatively undisturbed and well sealed. The spring/damper units were mounted outboard buried within the wheel rims, a feature which necessitated big, 19" diameter rear wheels. Tail bulges high enough to clear larger than standard rear tyres added drag.

With the underwing extending virtually to the entire planform area of the car side sealing was particularly significant. To continue the horizontal side skirts back as far as possible and to provide additional sealing the rear wheels were fully enclosed. The rear wheel covers clearly had to be detachable and although awkward for the mechanics were worth 10% of aerodynamic performance according to Southgate.

Front and rear wheel arches were brought as close as possible to the tyre and both ahead and behind the rear wheels the floor area spanned the gap between the base of the tail side panel and the base of the outer tunnel wall. It was not possible to 'blow' the diffuser tunnels in Formula One fashion since both primary and secondary exhaust pipe lengths were crucial to engine performance. The pipes exited over the tunnel roofs and pointed downwards to discharge into the diffuser wake. This kept the pipe ends to the regulation maximum height: Southgate denies any beneficial aerodynamic action was caused by the discharge. He points to an irony of the exit height regulation - had a side exit been possible the pipes could have discharged at any given height.

Understandably Southgate will not reveal aerodynamic performance figures for the XJR-6. However, it appears that the lift:drag ratio could be as high as 3.5:1 and we can assume that the XJR-6 at least matched the 4000lb. downforce figure quoted for the earlier Ford at maximum speed - say 180m.p.h. Indeed, it is likely that downforce in 'sprint' trim went well over twice the car's own weight at top speed - even the Porsche 956 could get well over one and a half times its own weight and it is clear that the XJR-6 very comfortably outperformed the German car on this score. And the XJR-6's aerodynamic split was in the region of 30 - 70 whereas that of the 956 was nearer to 20 - 80.

The high downforce produced by the XJR-6 was handled by an advanced composite tub reckoned to be at least 15 times stiffer than the Porsche's traditional sheet aluminium tub. Indeed, its torsional rigidity was so great that available measuring equipment was not man enough to deflect it. Essentially the monocoque was a big carbon fibre box, of which the large cross sectional area compared to a Formula One tub allowed Southgate to achieve exceptional stiffness. The ACT produced item was, however, somewhat over-engineered since, as we have noted, it represented a venture into virgin territory. "With the first car I could not be sure of the strength to weight ratio - if in doubt I made it too strong", Southgate admits. "It was therefore too heavy; I could chop the weight down without significant loss of structural rigidity".

Primarily the XJR-6 tub set carbon fibre skins over Nomex honeycomb. Naturally the number of layers and the weaves employed in the pre-preg skins varied according to application. The actual moulding process was not particularly involved since the tub was formed as a system of relatively flat sections, mostly in female tooling and each piece was small enough to slot inside the ACT autoclave. The vacuum pressure bonded, heat cured pieces were then cold bonded together with a two part adhesive. Around 20 major sections were assembled like a giant Airfix kit, the number of parts reflecting the extent and complexity of a prototype tub compared to a single seater tub.

The thickest, strongest part was the rear bulkhead which was carbon fibre over aluminium honeycomb. It had a forward projecting rim around its periphery, this flange adding significantly to rigidity while it also incorporated carbon blocks at stress points and Kevlar rods to spread the vertical loads. However, the structure was, Southgate says, strong enough without the rods. It contained no metal yet in a press recorded twice the FISA strength requirement for a roll hoop - without the Kevlar rods in place.

The only steel roll cage elements were a windscreen hoop (bonded to the pillars) and two tubes running back from that hoop across the roof to the top of the rear bulkhead. When the engine was in place, the roof tubes were linked to the cam covers via bolt-in engine bracing struts which located midway along the respective cam cover. At the front, since the engine slotted into a recess it was possible to bolt directly into each cam cover from above, down through the roof of the recess. Two lower longitudinal, horizontal bolts attached the sump. The back of the rear bulkhead was covered in aluminium foil to reflect heat, avoiding the danger of heat soak into the fuel tank.

The rear bulkhead had a separate carbon fibre

over Nomex fuel tank/ seat back moulding bonded to it. Underneath, the wide floor panel was a 50/50 carbon fibre/Kevlar skinned moulding which extended under the side boxes, the Kevlar weave offering tear and impact resistance. Kevlar was also used at the front of the side boxes, the portion facing the front wheels, for its resistance to stone damage. The side boxes were structural items, as were bulkheads at the dash and the front end. Other important structural items included the roof, an under-knee leg support panel which linked the side boxes across the cockpit floor, and a long panel extending from the dash to the front of the monocoque, forming the scuttle and enclosing the front suspension support assembly.

The front suspension was partially carried by a double bulkhead formed as two aluminium plates which were bolted into the advanced composite structure - the only major parts of the tub in metal. This bulkhead assembly straddled the front wheel axis and the pedals were fixed inside so the driver's feet reached just as far as it, staying within the wheelbase. Ahead, the master cylinders were enclosed by the composite front bulkhead, to which a composite nose box was bonded. Small magnesium castings were bolted inside the front corners of the monocoque to accept the leading front suspension pivots and spread the load. Use of magnesium rather than carbon for these pick ups eased manufacture.

The radiator was outrigged from the nose box, where it was encased by the nose and splitter. With scuttle, side box and roof shapes formed by the monocoque's outer surface, the nose, doors and tail were the only major body panels. The bodywork was formed of carbon fibre skins over Nomex honeycomb by ART, using pre-preg woven carbon bonded under vacuum pressure and cured under elevated temperature using a vacuum bag and large oven. Kevlar was again used for wear resistance inside the wheel arches.

The rear wing and diffuser tunnels were carbon fibre over Nomex honeycomb, again produced by ACT in its autoclave. Each wing element contained two transverse cross beams and four longitudinal formers, all in carbon fibre under a carbon fibre outer skin. The tunnels similarly needed to be rigid enough to hold shape in the face of strong aerodynamic forces and were in fact structural members, tying an aluminium rear suspension crossbeam to the rear of the monocoque.

The aluminium crossbeam straddled the gearbox and ran from wheel rim well to wheel rim well. At each end it supported the top of the respective spring/damper unit, which as we have noted was buried inside the rim out of the path of the tunnel. The crossbeam was positioned behind the upper wishbones (and associated track control arm), hence the spring/damper unit sat at the back of the upright (activated by a projection from its foot) leaving room for the (single four pot) caliper at the front.

The narrow based upper wishbone picked up at

the front of the upright, the t.c.a. at the rear, both accepted by a horizontal titanium (subsequently steel) pin that passed right through the top of the magnesium alloy casting. The base of the upright was carried by a wide based lower wishbone. The supporting rod end was received by a threaded bush on the wishbone so that it could be screwed in or out to provide camber adjustment, while the t.c.a.'s rod ends controlled toe in. Once the camber setting was fixed the very heavily loaded lower wishbone's rod end could be locked via a pinchbolt, the bush having been split to allow the pinchbolt facility.

As *Racecar Engineering* contributor Allan Staniforth has pointed out (in *Race Tech: Suspension-* GT Foulis 1988/ ISBN 0 85429 645 X), another designer would have utilised a locknut and a threaded sleeve within the main bush to allow length adjustment to a much finer degree than the half a thread available with the pinchbolt. However, the tightening of the locknut introduces a stress line into the base of one of the threads and Southgate's alternative avoided that at this crucial point. It took more time to make, cost a degree of fine adjustment but gave a tiny amount of extra strength: extra reliability.

A steel anti roll bar ran along the aluminium crossbeam with arms reaching forward to pick up on the uprights. The rear uprights were cast by Kent Aerospace Castings then machined by TCP while the wishbones were fabricated from 41/30 steel by TCP. The wishbone supports were provided by the transaxle assembly. The uprights carried "second generation" ball bearings, two sets of races forming a compact, light assembly with a small hub of maraging steel. The disc bell - aluminium alloy - and wheel were driven by four titanium pegs. A heat shield was positioned between the back of the disc and adjacent coil spring/damper unit. Fixed rate titanium springs and Bilstein (non adjustable) gas dampers were specified.

The entire upright - brake - spring/damper assembly could be housed within a 19" rim of 15 $^1$/4" width without exaggerating the wheel offset. The big diameter rim was a specially commissioned one piece magnesium casting from Speedline in Italy and carried Dunlop Denloc tyres. Denloc is a system to keep the bead in place in the event of a puncture: it is when the bead collapses into the well that the driver finds it hardest to control the car.

At the front Denlocs ran on 12" wide, 17" diameter Speedlines. The front suspension featured upper and (wider based) lower wishbones and pushrod coil spring/damper operation. The dampers were located under the scuttle sandwiched high between the aluminium bulkhead plates and lying in a near horizontal position with their heads sharing a central locating lug. This general arrangement had previously been employed by Southgate at the front of a Cosworth Ford-Osella Formula One car. However, in the Osella application the pushrod compressed the spring/damper unit directly which gave a 2:1 ratio between wheel movement and spring/damper movement. In view of that, Southgate introduced a rocking arm between the pushrod and the spring/damper unit to provide a variable ratio.

The push rod operated front suspension arrangement added a little extra weight and complexity but offered a number of advantages. The spring/damper unit location was structurally sound, the central lug spreading the load, while the dampers were easily accessible for adjustment and well clear of brake ducting while the pushrods eased suspension setting.

The system offered very slight rising rate: with less than 2" wheel movement rate changes were not of particular significance. The car was designed to be run as low (and consistently low) as possible at the front for aerodynamic reasons. Due to the width of the tub more ground clearance had to be provided than for a ground effect single seater and Southgate admits that it was a case of 'as low as we dare'. For this reason, the entire front structure was designed to rub and to survive! A Koni gas/fluid adjustable damper was run inside a titanium fixed rate spring: the Koni was faster reacting than the Bilstein and offered harder settings if less ride comfort.

The front suspension worked in conjunction with a conventional anti roll bar - a steel bar ran across the front bulkhead with arms reaching back to pick up on the lower wishbone via a short link which kept the bar high enough to avoid the radiator plumbing. The steering rack was inside the front bulkhead and the steering arms picked up on the front of the cast magnesium upright. Again the upright was from KAC via TCP while the steering was Jack Knight rack and pinion in a TWR case. The steering provided 1.5 turns lock to lock and while it picked up on the front of the upright the (again four pot, single) caliper trailed to allow room for brake cooling ducting. Due to lack of time for detail design, the ducting was straightforward and did not feed through the back of the upright.

Front and rear discs were cross drilled AP Racing 13" curved vane and were gripped by Ferodo DS11 pads. The pads fitted into conventional four pot AP Racing calipers, these having two aluminium halves bolted together with steel bolts. Each caliper was bolted to its respective upright via a mounting lug. Both front and rear discs were driven through aluminium bells by titanium pegs and the rear hubs were turned by solid 1" diameter maraging steel driveshafts through GKN c.v. joints. Inner and outer joints were conventional GKN c.v.s and thanks to the 19" rims the driveshafts sloped upwards, working at a significant angle which was not in the best interest of c.v. longevity.

The power came from a Salisbury-type differential while the gearbox was a March 85T, driven by an AP triple plate clutch of the conventional 7$^1$/4 inch gear driven type. The bellhousing was cast magnesium alloy and set the engine 230mm. ahead of the gearbox main case. The clutch operating mechanism was kept on top to ease access and with the oil tank elsewhere the bellhousing was empty save for the clutch, the clutch shaft and a shaft support bearing. At the back it formed prominent 'ears' to support the front of the upper wishbone assembly (the back of that assembly was supported by the crossbeam) and it also carried the pick up for the forward leg of the lower wishbone.

The March gearbox was chosen since the Hewland VG was not considered sufficiently reliable and TWR did not have the time to develop its own 'box. The March 85T (a sportscar version of an Indy car 'box) was similar in general terms to the VG but the magnesium alloy main case split transversely at the rear axle line to allow installation of a larger, stronger c.w.p. Additionally, between the rear portion of the main case and the bearing carrier was a 'strap' to provide additional shaft support, again adding to the strength of the unit. The strap piece set an additional bearing on each shaft run, and four of the gears lay ahead of it, two behind. The bearing carrier was of the Hewland DG pattern and the gearbox layout and operation was typical Hewland. Staffs Silent Gear Co. gears were run and the 'box was prepared by Roni, which also looked after the differential.

The case was run unmodified and blocks were bolted to its standard lugs to hold the suspension and crossbeam mounts. However, a TWR endplate was fitted to carry the rear air jack and the aluminium plate-type wing supports. On board air jacks were run front and rear, with a jack located behind each front wheel. A novel accessory was a gearbox temperature gauge on the dashboard.

Transmission cooling was via a radiator atop the gearbox (just behind the rear deck). There was no engine oil radiator, instead a heat exchanger was conveniently situated under the oil tank in a pipe servicing the front located Serck water radiator. The nose inlet fed both the water radiator and the front brakes, while the only other air inlets were NACA ducts in the rear deck which supplied cooling air for the rear brakes.

There was no engine air scoop - the trumpets were left to breathe through an aperture cut in the dorsum. Since the Lucas starter motor was positioned right at the front of the engine it sat within the monocoque recess, keeping well out of the way of the diffuser tunnels. The Varley battery was carried in the righthand side box while the spark box was just inside the engine bay, hung on the rear bulkhead, and the Zytek box was kept well away from it, housed in the cockpit on the back of the passenger seat.

The fuel tank carried three Premier fuel cells, one behind the seats, two other smaller ones in the side boxes. This arrangement was attended by a host of pumps, the complexity of the system another reflection of the lack of time for detail design. Fuel consumption was monitored by a TWR/Zytek digital system based on a count of injector pulses. The pulses from one injector were recorded and this reading was multiplied by 12 to derive total injector opening time. Since the fuel pressure was kept constant the consumption could be accurately calculated and the driver was informed of litres consumed and number of laps available on the fuel remaining at the current rate of consumption, information he could compare to the pit board showing laps left to run.

The dashboard instruments were supplied by Smiths, conventional oil and water temperature gauges flanking the rev counter immediately ahead of the driver. Ahead of the passenger seat were fuel and oil pressure gauges and a volt meter while warning lights facing the driver indicated low oil and fuel pressure. The car was equipped with a pits/driver radio link - as the Group A5 XJ-S had been - primarily for use as a tactical weapon.

The driver sat directly against the tank/seat back moulding restrained by Willans belts. Two Lifeline extinguisher bottles - one discharging into the cockpit, the other into the engine trumpets - were positioned at the foot of the passenger space. The windscreen was a Triplex laminated glass/plastic sandwich with a 2.5mm. thick glass outer layer, a wafer thin 0.1mm. plastic interlayer and a 1.5mm. glass inner layer. It was swept by a single Trico wiper blade. The cockpit was accessed by gullwing doors carrying perspex windows. The nose was equipped with single Cibie headlights while the tail carried Land Rover based light assemblies.

# The Boxer Beat

Early Eighties Group C racing was dominated by one marque: Porsche. The Stuttgart firm sold customer versions of its car, backed by a full service operation, and the few races that didn't fall to the Rothmans supported factory team were picked up by 'Porschesport's' customers. Yet the all conquering 956 chassis (and the longer wheelbase 962C version introduced for 1985 to conform to the new feet behind the front wheel axis ruling) was powered by an engine derived from the classic air cooled Porsche 901 engine of the early Sixties, which in turn had been heavily influenced by the VW Beetle.

The Beetle was, of course, the brainchild of Professor Ferdinand Porsche, father of Ferdinand and Louise who founded the family marque. For years Porsche road cars were powered by tuned Beetle engines and when Porsche designed a six cylinder replacement for its Sixties sports cars it retained the characteristic 'boxer' configuration and air cooling.

The original 2.0 litre 901 engine had individual aluminium heads on individual Biral cylinder barrels bolted either side of an aluminium crankcase cum sump that split vertically into symmetrical halves. Biral was a combination of an iron liner fixed in an aluminium sleeve, the latter forming the cooling fins. The separate heads on each side were joined by a magnesium cam box that carried a s.o.h.c. chain driven off the front end from a layshaft running under the relatively high mounted crankshaft and geared to it. The short layshaft was supported by two bearings and a shaft was screwed into the back of it to drive the oil pump which was situated at the back of the centrally scavenged sump.

Each camshaft actuated two valves per cylinder through rockers to allow the valves to be disposed either side of the cylinder axis in a hemispherical combustion chamber. The piston crown was domed to match (with light valve clearance notches) forming a classic 'orange peel' chamber. Ignition was via a single plug per cylinder while each cylinder was fed through its own Solex carburettor. The inlet manifold fed down into the head with the exhaust tucked underneath the engine.

Conventional reciprocating parts drove an eight bearing steel crankshaft, each con rod having its own pin and there being an additional bearing to steady the layshaft drive gear and to provide an oil feed to the crankshaft. The crankpins were disposed so that adjacent pairs were at 180 degrees to each other and thus opposing pairs of pistons 'boxed' towards and away from each other. This made for a well balanced engine with full exhaust tuning potential. The disadvantage was excessive inner turbulence and compression which sapped a significant amount of power.

On the nose of the crankshaft was a pulley which drove the belt powering the fan which had the alternator mounted in its hub. The fan was vertically mounted ahead of the cylinders with g.r.p. ducting to direct air to the barrels and the generously finned heads, VW Beetle style. Power was spent driving the fan but did not have to be spent pushing a water radiator through the air. However, a generous oil radiator was required, the engine relying perhaps 30% upon oil for cooling.

Porsche went endurance racing with a 'supertuned' version of the 901 engine in the Carrera 6 of 1966. This had chrome plated bores in all-aluminium cylinders, a lightweight magnesium crankcase, forged alloy pistons driving titanium rods, twin plug heads and Kugelfischer mechanical injection. The Porsche flat six had been designed to be rugged and to allow for future capacity increases. In the Seventies it went to just over 3.0 litres and in the mid Seventies a four valve derivative was designed. For this it was necessary to water cool the heads since there was no longer enough room for air to circulate properly. The four valve version was turbocharged from the outset: Porsche had pioneered this technology since 1971. Indeed, it was turbocharging that had kept its two valve 'boxer' engine alive in international endurance racing.

The early Seventies turbocharged version of the two valve 901 engine had Nikasil cylinders (all-aluminium cylinders with a nickel-silicon carbide bore coating) bolted to its magnesium crankcase and adopted a Bosch CD system to fire twin plugs but otherwise retained the characteristics of the Carrera 6 engine of 1966 and in 2.1 litre guise even had the same 66mm. stroke steel crank, and borrowed Carrera 6 con rods. The most obvious concessions to turbocharging were the fitting of a cylinder head O-ring seal and sodium cooled valves, Nimonic on the exhaust side. The output of the cooling fan was also stepped up and later versions were equipped with a horizontal fan, driven through the usual belt then a pair of shafts connected via bevel gears. In this case the alternator was mounted on its own bracket and had its own drivebelt.

At first the compression ratio had been lowered

*Amazingly Porsche dominated Group C racing from its inception in 1982 right up until the mid Eighties with this cooling fan equipped boxer engine. The four valve Typ 935 engine was air, oil and water cooled with additional air:air aftercooling for its charge air.*

to 6.5:1 and up to 2.4 bar pressure had been felt in a single central plenum thanks to a single KKK turbocharger which blew through an air:air aftercooler. Each cylinder's intake pipe had its own butterfly valve and a single injector, Bosch mechanical injection again employed with the pump now made sensitive to boost pressure as well as throttle opening and revs. The early 2.1 litre engine had been rated 490b.h.p./7,600r.p.m. at 2.35 bar.

At the end of '74 Porsche had launched a turbocharged '930' road car as the homologated base model from which a silhouette (Group 5) racer could be derived. The 930 had a 3.0 litre engine with a 70.4mm. stroke and this was combined with a 92.8mm. bore for the Group 5 racer to provide a capacity of 2856cc. - just under 4.0 litres given FISA's 1.4 times equivalency factor. The only major departure from the original turbocharged race engine (aside from displacement) was an aluminium crankcase. As loadings increased, magnesium had been found wanting.

The so called Typ 930/72 twin plug engine of the 935, again with mechanical injection system and CD ignition, was rated over 600b.h.p. and that was unaffected by an early switch to water:air aftercooling as dictated by a FISA ruling. A twin turbocharged version followed for improved throttle response. It officially produced 630b.h.p./ 8,000r.p.m. on a safe 2.4 bar absolute plenum pressure. Subsequent Group 5 developments included the introduction of the gear driven four valve engine with water cooled heads and this was the basis of the Eighties Group C engine.

Hans Mezger designed the more exotic derivative of the Typ 901. In fact, he drew a gear driven four valve engine in five possible displacements ranging from 1.4 to 3.2 litres. The first built was the biggest version, codenamed Typ 935/71. This had an even larger capacity than that of the existing 935 (Typ 930/72): 3211cc. This was achieved through the use of the 74.4mm. crankshaft together with a bigger, 95.7mm. bore.

The new (individual) four valve water cooled heads were welded to the cylinder barrels, overcoming any potential gasket problem. Two valve heads could not have been welded in place since it would have been impossible to insert the valves. The new (single central plug) head featured a narrow valve angle (30 degrees included) and was run together with flat top pistons. The inlet valve was set at 14 degrees from the cylinder axis, the exhaust at 16 degrees.

The cylinders were still Nikasil and the production aluminium crankcase was retained, although with provision for larger main bearings and larger crankpins. A new magnesium cam box carried twin camshafts per bank which actuated the valves through conventional steel bucket tappets. The revised turbo engine was designed for 9,000r.p.m. operation and was gear driven with, in effect, two intermediate gears (mounted on plain bearings) replacing each chain.

Since it now cooled only the cylinder barrels, the fan was again vertical, as usual belt driven off the nose of the crank. It was smaller in diameter, absorbing far less power, and with all its output directed on the cylinders these ran cooler. Again the alternator was mounted on its own bracket and was belt driven from the fan drive pulley.

Each bank of heads had its own water cooling system with the pump driven off the front of the respective exhaust cam. The CD trigger was now mounted on the rear of the righthand intake camshaft rather than the crankshaft for less vibration while the distributor was positioned symmetrically on the opposite bank. The twin turbo 935/71 engine of 1976 ran a 7.0:1 compression ratio and was reckoned to produce the power of the two-valver at 0.15 bar less boost. Standard manifold pressure soon became 2.5 bar and at that the engine was rated 750 b.h.p./8,200 r.p.m. while at 2.7 bar qualifying pressure it offered around 800 b.h.p.

Concurrently with the 3211.0cc. engine Porsche devised a 2140.0cc. (3.0 litre FISA equivalent) four valve Sports-Prototype engine (935/73), essentially similar, and this offered 580 b.h.p./8,500 r.p.m. at 2.5 bar absolute and 625 b.h.p. in qualifying pumping 2.7 bar. Then came 935/72 - a 2650.0cc. derivative with single turbocharger and without aftercooler as per Indy Car regulations. However, since the oval racer ran on alcohol Porsche was able to dispense with the cooling fan. Engine Typ 935/72 had the classic 66mm. stroke crankshaft together with a 92.3mm. bore (for 2649.65cc.) and, with a compression ratio of 9.0:1 was rated 630 b.h.p. at 9,000 r.p.m. on the USAC regulation maximum 2.03 bar absolute.

Although stillborn, the 2.65 litre engine was perceived as having the ideal capacity for a twin turbocharged unit to meet the requirements of Group C. Thus the combination of 66mm. crankshaft and 92.3mm. bore surfaced at Le Mans rather than Indianapolis. The 935/76 engine for Porsche's 1982-launched 956 sports-prototype was first race-tested at Le Mans in '81, then its specification was finalised.

The 935/76 Group C engine remained essentially to the specification of the 935/71 unit, with twin KKK turbochargers (one per bank) and Bosch mechanical injection (one injector per cylinder) and CD ignition, but it ran air:air aftercoolers, one for each bank (each having its own plenum chamber). Of course, the familiar vertical fan seemed somewhat incongruous in a state of the art Eighties Sports-Prototype! The compression ratio was set at 7.2:1 and (given Group C fuel consumption regulations) on a typical 2.2 bar race boost power was quoted as 620 b.h.p./8,200 r.p.m. with maximum revs of 8,400 r.p.m.

Development of the Group C engine saw the introduction in 1983 of the Bosch Motronic engine management system which allowed the compression ratio to rise, first to 8.0:1, then 8.5:1 over the '83 season, power rising to 650 b.h.p. without an increase in race boost. For 1984 the ratio went to 9.0:1. With the Motronic system the Group C engine was known as the Typ 935/82. Pioneered by the factory team, it was offered to Porsche's many 956 customers from 1984 onwards. Nevertheless, some customers, including Joest

Racing, preferred to continue with the higher pressure mechanical injection which offered superior atomisation, particularly as Porsche insisted on customers running factory-supplied EPROM chips.

Both electronic and mechanical engines could easily be converted to larger displacements - ranging from 2.8 to 3.2 litres - but the factory retained 2.65 litres into '85 if some privateers - including Joest and Fitzpatrick - are known to have tried larger capacity engines. Generally the privateers and the factory team shared the same aluminium monocoque chassis but Richard Lloyd Racing sought an advantage from its own stiffer aluminium honeycomb tub which was run with a modified front suspension and AP four pot brakes rather than the regular twin two pot Ate items. Nevertheless, other than at Le Mans in 1985 where Joest Racing humbled it with a superficially standard 956, the factory retained an iron grip on Group C.

Surprisingly, the 1981 conceived 956 chassis represented Porsche's first venture into monocoque technology. It was also its first ground effect car and had been developed by a team led by Norbert Singer using 20% scale models in Porsche's own fixed floor wind tunnel.

The 956 monocoque ran from pedal box to firewall bulkhead with an integral central fuel tank, the driver's feet positioned ahead of the front wheel axis. The sheet metal structure carried a light alloy roll cage and was fully shrouded by bodywork. Behind, the engine was semi stressed, steel A-frames running back to pick up on the transaxle. Both the engine and transaxle were tilted upwards at five degrees to make room for the diffuser upsweep. Since the engine was short, to achieve a 40 - 60 weight distribution a long bellhousing cum spacer was set between it and Porsche's own gearbox which, typically, put the c.w.p. at the front of the main case. A hatch in the side of the bellhousing facilitated clutch removal.

The aluminium bellhousing and magnesium gearbox castings were carefully shaped to pick up the engine support A-frames and to carry the rear suspension which set the coil spring/damper units in a vee formation above the c.w.p. housing to avoid encroaching upon the diffuser upsweep. The angled drivetrain and the use of 16" rear rims ensured a horizontal driveshaft line. The drive was from a spool - in other words there was no differential action - while the gearbox was of the archetypal Hewland pattern but featured Porsche syncromesh. This slowed changes but helped promote Porsche's syncromesh patent which was licensed throughout the world. Porsche gearbox reliability was well proven, even in 1000 b.h.p. Can Am turbocars.

The coil spring/damper units over the main case were operated by triangulated tubular structures atop the upper wishbone. The springs were titanium while the dampers were Bilstein gas units. The front suspension likewise incorporated Bilstein gas dampers and these - again with co-axial springs - were outboard on the traditional pattern. The coils wrapping them were again titanium and were of taper wire and varying wind to provide a measure of progressive rate, a trick long used by Porsche. Rack and pinion steering was employed and conventional anti roll bars were fitted front and rear.

The front suspension was supported by the front of the compact monocoque, to which an aluminium nose box was attached. The monocoque sides were formed by torsion boxes but these did not reach the full width of the car: additional bonded-on plastic side sponsons were outrigged. The sponsons reached door sill height and the water, oil and aftercoolers were mounted upon them in a mid position flanking the fuel tank. The cooler feed was taken through the horizontal section of the door and hot air was extracted through the tail, up over the rear wheel arch.

Under the cooler exit channels (in detachable rear sections of the sponsons) were the turbochargers, conveniently flanking the engine and situated close to the aftercoolers. In turn the aftercoolers were close to the plenum chambers, minimising the length of charge plumbing to the benefit of response. The single turbocharger per bank exhausted through the respective tail flank. The engine fan was fed via a NACA duct in the roof. With all coolers mid mounted the only ducts in the concave nose were for brake cooling - these flanking the underswept entrance to the underwing - and cockpit cooling.

The bodywork was of Kevlar reinforced g.r.p. over aluminium honeycomb and only roof, windscreen and side boxes were non detachable.

There was a choice of long or short tail, each to be run with its own nose under-profile and rear underbody. In both cases the wing was mounted on fins above the rear deck, partly outrigged in the case of the higher downforce, higher drag short tail option which shared the same overall length.

As we have noted, the underwing took the form of a central channel running from nose funnel to diffuser exit and there was an indentation in the monocoque floor to offer more depth than would have been provided by ground clearance alone. The central channel exceeded the width of the mandatory flat plate, all but filling the gap between the wheels and the diffuser upsweep commenced right behind the 'plate'. The width of the engine restricted diffuser design, hence a relatively long and gentle upsweep under a tilted drivetrain. This, of course, was interrupted only by the bulge needed to clear the gearbox as the diffuser approached the rear while the underbody engine air extractor vents robbed potential downforce.

Interestingly, between the front wheels was a transverse underbody indent. This caused a local slowing of the airflow while the portion of the underwing immediately behind the nose funnel then effectively led into a primary venturi throat. Apparently, this concept was a creed of the German school of underwing design - Southgate recalls that the idea was proposed to him while he worked in the Ford Cologne wind tunnel during development of the Ford Group C design in 1982.

It appears that the 956/962C had an inherent aerodynamic split in the region of 20 - 80 front - rear and some privateers fitted an ungainly wing above the nose for slow circuits where good turn in was particularly important. A 'guestimate' of

*The traditional way of constructing a race car monocoque - heat and metal combine to produce a sheet alloy structure reinforced with alloy tubes. This was new age technology for Porsche in the early Eighties since right until 1981 it had run spaceframe cars.*

downforce for the car in regular trim is one and threequarters its own weight at maximum speed, reducing to one and a half times its own weight for a long tail car at Le Mans flat out on the Mulsanne. Top speed was in the region of 230m.p.h., while the Le Mans lift: drag ratio appears to have been in the region of 2.5:1.

The 956 ran on Denloc shod BBS modular (magnesium centre/ aluminium inner and outer section) rims, 16" both front and rear and incorporating extractor fans to draw hot air from the brakes. The outboard brakes from Ate (another German supplier) were twin two pot calipers over 13" diameter cross drilled, ventilated cast iron discs. The 956 weighed in at the minimum 850kg., as did the 962 in spite of a wheelbase lengthened from 2650mm. to 2770mm. thanks to the lengthened tub necessary to push the front wheel axis ahead of the pedals. The Porsche 956/962C chassis running the Typ 935/82 engine was used by all serious regular runners in the '85 World Endurance Championship - aside from the works Lancia team. The twin turbocharged 3.0 litre V8 propelled Lancia LC2 was fleet but the Italian factory team rarely got its act together. Porsche technology had been the class of '82 and was still in charge in '85...

*Wind tunnel model of the projected 956 shape - note undercut nose funneling air to the central underwing. Porsche employed fixed floor wind tunnel testing until forced to update to rolling road tests by 1987 humilation on the Indy Car scene. The 1982-launched 956 (illustrated in cutaway and on track photograph right) lacked opposition able to exploit its weak chassis design until the arrival of TWR.*

# Back to Mosport

Mosport Park had been the scene of Bob Tullius' first professional racing venture for Jaguar: the start of the V12 campaign that would take Group 44 to Le Mans. Nine years later, it would see the launch of the TWR sports-prototype programme. While Group 44 was making its second Le Mans bid in June 1985, over in Kidlington TWR Racing Manager Roger Silman was co-ordinating the build programme for the first XJR-6 chassis. Having commenced in February, the completed car was ready for a shakedown at Snetterton in early July. Martin Brundle, a driver with the Tyrrell Grand Prix team, took the controls and went two seconds a lap quicker than he had previously managed with TWR's four valve engined XJR-5 test car.

Silman recalls: "the car showed enormous potential. However, it was immediately apparent that the lead time was too short. The car wasn't 100% and that was directly attributable to the short time in which it had been built".

On the other hand, had the car been built more slowly it wouldn't have been ready for a significant race programme in '85 and the '86 campaign couldn't have been launched on the back of solid Group C competition experience. Snetterton had been chosen as the launch venue on the basis of UK circuit availability and its rough surface was likely to highlight any weakness of the new design. The subsequent strip down revealed a clean bill of health.

The prototype next tested at Donington Park the following week, just a couple of days before qualifying for the Hockenheim 1000km. race. With insufficient spare parts available as yet there was no question of the car being shipped to Germany. Indeed, it was still awaiting its distinctive rear wheel covers. An early problem was a lack of cooling capacity and this had quickly seen the heat exchanger replaced by a Setrab oil radiator positioned low in the flank of the lefthand side of the engine bay, just behind the oil tank. Opposite, a small lightweight aluminium VW water radiator in the flank of the righthand side assisted water cooling. Each cooler was served by a small scoop projecting from the respective tail side panel.

A more significant problem at this early stage was harnessing the potential cornering performance. Silman: "the car was extremely good aerodynamically but Tony was somewhat surprised by the chassis specification required to make the most of its potential. The challenge of '85 was one of trying to evolve a chassis specification to match the aerodynamics".

That was a challenge for Dunlop as well as TWR. The aerodynamic loading imparted by the very effective new ground effect car was territory unexplored by Dunlop, well outside its experience with Porsche. The car was also heavy, weighing in at just over 900kg. And it understeered. Southgate recalls: "on its first run it understeered like hell! It took a month to get it into shape".

The fundamental problem was the effect of carrying a heavy engine with a high centre of gravity. The XJR-6 had been blessed with good front-rear weight distribution and high downforce and enjoyed plenty of traction and impressive grip. However, initially its performance was biased towards the rear, mainly due to the effect of its unwieldy V12 lump wallowing around in the back.

When a race car has bags of downforce the driver turns in very quickly: a ground effect car can be thrown into a corner with an aplomb that would be highly dangerous in a conventional car. The ground effect machine doesn't go out of control since it is being squashed into the ground by its own massive download. However, the dynamic weight transfer is massive. Throwing a Group C car into a corner causes a severe diagonal pitch across its weighty chassis. And the XJR-6 was not only heavy, it also had a high centre of gravity. That was found to vault the sudden weight transfer to an alarming degree. As Southgate puts it - something had to prop it up!

In theory, such a prop could be stiff front springs or a stiff front anti roll bar. Stiff springs affect a car all around the circuit whereas clearly a stiff anti roll is felt only in the corners. At this stage it might be worth briefly highlighting the role of an anti roll bar. The bar resists roll, and also acts like an extra spring added to the existing ones, particularly at the outer wheel. The car sees it partially as an extra spring and it can provide effects far more powerful than fitting harder springs. Also, it moves weight from the inner to the outer wheel and the combined effect of front and rear bars can move weight off the front and onto the rear, and vice versa.

The XJR-6 ran stiff front springs from the outset. Intentionally, there was only an inch or so wheel movement, around half of which was provided by tyre wall flexibility. Minimal movement kept the fat tyres stable and reduced potential suspension problems while helping minimise pitch and roll to the benefit of the operation of the underwing.

Effective ground effect cars tend to run very hard at the front. However, as it was progressively

*The XJR-6 commenced testing in the summer of '85 without rear wheel covers (to which Southgate credits 10% of its performance). Note also lack of louvers over front wheel arch cutouts. At this stage the car was bugged by understeer...*

dialled in the XJR-6 had to have its front anti roll bar stiffened to a surprising and abnormal degree. In crude terms, as performance was extracted from the machine it became imperative to fit a big bar at the front to stop it burying itself in the ground. In this respect it was important that the chassis was stiff and could support very heavy bar loadings without bending. Only a fractional deflection by suspension points can make a mockery of precise wheel control.

The process of sorting the new design was clearly an involved one and as it grappled with the early understeer problem, for slower circuits TWR grafted on a nose wing. Such an aerodynamic fix for a problem of mechanical grip was inappropriate and thus strictly temporary. Meanwhile, Dunlop toiled to develop a taller, wider front tyre. At the same time the team methodically ascended its steep learning curve, the prototype undergoing many more test miles. In late July Mike Thackwell managed to get within half a second of the Silverstone Group C lap record on race tyres, still without rear wheel covers and the taller, wider fronts. The potential was obvious.

By early August a second chassis had been finished, this reckoned to be somewhat lighter though still over 890kg. The two cars were promptly shipped to Canada for the 1000km. race at Mosport, the newcomer thus having its shakedown at the circuit the day before qualifying commenced. Remember, this was only six months from the start of the prototype build programme.

The British racing green machines weighed in at 910kg. (001 - Brundle/Thackwell) and 895 kg. (002 - Hans Heyer/ Jean-Louis Schlesser). For the bumpy, tight track TWR had fitted steel springs and a spoiler lip on the back of the concave nose panel (ahead of the radiator exit), with its temporary nose wing above. There were rear wheel covers for the first time.

*Autosport* reported: "During practice the team experimented with all the permutations offered by an extra nose wing and the rear wheel covers, aligned with adjustments to the regular aerodynamic package... However, not even all this and the usual compromises of springs, roll bars and ride height could entirely rid the cars of understeer as the drivers came off the brakes in some of the turns and got on the throttle. This characteristic quickly rooted the front tyres, and the extra wing made the situation worse. Finally it was decided to run without the wing pending the arrival of wider fronts getting more rubber onto the road. These arrived from England during the second qualifying session, and produced an immediate improvement".

The new tyres were 25mm. taller as well as 20mm. wider than the fronts the car had been designed to run. They made the car heavier to drive but improved handling and enhanced stopping power. Nevertheless, tyre life on the abrasive circuit continued to render qualifying tyres useless. On soft race rubber Brundle cut a best XJR-6 lap of 1m 12.602s compared to a hard-trying pole position time of 1m 09.775s for the turbo boosted works Porsche team. Porsche expressed surprise at the qualifying speed of the Jaguars which lined up third and fifth on the grid sandwiching the fastest private Porsche. However, aside from the Weissach based cars there was precious little opposition.

Brundle made a superb start to snatch the lead and he held the two works Porsches at bay for ten glorious laps. The German cars needed a squirt of extra boost to get past. Brundle then found he could shadow them... only to retire at the end of lap 13, the front left wheelbearing having failed. The problem was caused by a detail of the upright and hub assembly design which was subsequently modified.

Brundle and Thackwell were switched to the second car, putting Heyer out of work for the day, and soon this entry lost three minutes while Schlesser had a front wheel vibration checked. All was well and 001 finished third, in spite of a stop for a new front brake caliper then a valve spring failure during the late stages. Valve spring development was, as yet, unavoidably lagging. The massive acceleration and high lift imparted to the valve of a normally aspirated two valve race engine gives its springs a very hard time. Scott had designed a new spring for the Group C V12 but this could not be readied before '86 - an 'interim' spring had to be run through '85.

Of Mosport Silman reflects: "it was a nightmare. We simply weren't ready". The lessons? "We felt sure we had the ingredients to do the job, it was a matter of sorting the details. With hundreds of items to attend to that was no easy task".

The team's first European outing was on the magnificent high speed Spa Francorchamps circuit, for which it was safe to re-fit titanium springs. The wheelbearing support had been duly strengthened and a remoulded nose was evident. The front wing had gone and the subtly revised nose set a moulded lip ahead of the radiator exit. It was flanked by narrow raked bibs projecting ahead of the front wheel arches. At the rear there was enlarged brake ducting.

The opposition this time included two works Lancias as well as a stronger line up of factory and private Porsches with the Joest, Lloyd, Kremer and Brun teams all present. The fast, sweeping nature of the circuit favoured turbocharged qualifying power and the Jaguars lined up eighth (Brundle/Thackwell) and 11th (Heyer/Schlesser). Although even the faster Jaguar was over four seconds off pole TWR was confident of a good race pace. In fact, the car turned out to be "undriveable" on race day. It was a chassis problem that Silman will not reveal - "it took a while to establish but once established it was quickly rectified and didn't recur".

Schlesser/Heyer hit problems early on and retired with differential failure while after 50 long laps Brundle was sixth but a lap down. The lead car finished fifth two laps down in a race shortened to five hours following an accident that claimed the

life of Porsche driver Stefan Bellof. Bellof had been Brundle's Tyrrell teammate and Ken Tyrrell withdrew the Englishman from further sports-prototype competition. Jan Lammers was drafted in to replace Brundle at Brands Hatch while Alan Jones took over from Thackwell who had a clashing Formula 3000 commitment.

Brands Hatch saw further experimentation with the nose wing in view of the sinuous nature of the circuit and revised front brake ducts. Following

*Mosport Park in 1985 was the stage for the launch of a project that would eventually give Jaguar a victory at Le Mans using a V12 engine designed three*

*decades earlier. Unlike the contemporary Aston Martin V8 stock block engined cars, the stock block propelled TWR Group C challenger was highly effective.*

further wind tunnel work the rear deck had been shortened around 150mm. (so that the rear panel was angled forward rather than vertical) and the wing had been moved forward to maintain the crucial deck/wing relationship. The new arrangement had worked better in the tunnel, says Southgate. Another fundamental change saw revised front and rear anti roll bar layouts for shorter, stiffer bar arms. The front bar was progressively getting stiffer...

The two Jaguars were qualified by Jones and Lammers and were raced by Jones/Schlesser and Lammers/Heyer. The principal opposition on home soil consisted of two Lancias and three works Porsches, one with an experimental PDK (clutchless-operation) gearbox, Porsche privateers absent on this occasion. Although the XJR-6s were again over four seconds off pole, the team was once more confident of a strong race showing. Alas, both cars were hampered by tyres turning on the rim and early on Jones suffered a stuck throttle and the engine was wrecked. In the wake of the

tyre problem the Lammers car settled into fifth place a lap down but just short of two hours dropped a valve. Another manifestation of the valve spring problem.

Valve spring and circlip failures bugged qualifying for Fuji, the penultimate race of the season. Engine problems and a large contingent of powerful Nissan and Toyota turbocars as well as a large fleet of Porsches kept the Jaguars, driven here by Thackwell with Formula 3000 teammate John Nielsen and Heyer with saloon racer Steve Soper, down to 19th and 20th position on the grid. This was the race from which all the European runners withdrew in the face of a washed out track and the two XJR-6s - now with NACA ducts in the spats to help reduce rear tyre temperatures - were shipped straight to Malaysia for the Selangor 800.

There was still no spare car since the team had not yet had the opportunity to build up the 385 monocoque. Meanwhile, 185 and 285 had gained a little weight: race cars invariably get heavier rather than lighter with development (unless the development is specifically to save weight). Nevertheless, the Shah Alam circuit near Kuala Lumpur offered tight corners that favoured the instant response and torque of Scott's V12 engine and the improving grip and handling of Southgate's stiff, high downforce chassis.

With a now extremely stiff front end plus rapidly accumulating practical experience understeer was well under control - the chassis performance was starting to match the aerodynamic potential. Lammers managed the first 100m.p.h. lap of the Micky Mouse venue. He told *Autosport*: "the car now does everything we ask of it. Braking, turn in, balance, grip, acceleration - all are absolutely right".

Of course, the XJR-6 was still handicapped by its weight and the team still had no answer for turbo qualifying power (nor a spare car allowing the drivers to take risks). The meeting pitted Jaguar against five Porsches (three privately entered) and although Porsche turbo muscle eventually told, Thackwell (sharing again with Nielsen) qualified less than 1.5 seconds off pole in fourth position while Lammers, this time sharing with Gianfranco Brancatelli, was fifth.

The race saw Lammers forge ahead of Thackwell and Stuck's works Porsche to run second to Ickx' works car... only to spin into early retirement as a tyre threw a tread. Thackwell came in prematurely, badly affected by the tropical heat. Neither he nor Nielsen could run a full stint. The race was dominated by the sole surviving of the two works Porsches but, with Lammers drafted in to help, the surviving Jaguar came from three laps down at mid distance to finish one lap adrift of a cruising victor.

It hadn't been enough just to be second - the team had needed to close the gap as far as possible to make it a psychologically uplifting second place. Which it had done by gambling on the fuel, finishing with just a few drops to spare.

*TWR's exciting new XJR-6 Group C car first raced on home soil at Brands Hatch in 1985. Victory would have been rather too much to have hoped for after only two races abroad: the show was spectacular but short. A few races later Britain would witness a very different outcome...*

# Target 700b.h.p.

When Allan Scott had designed the TWR Group C engine in '83/'84 the Porsche Typ 935/81 engine was giving a maximum 650b.h.p. race power from 2.65 litres. However, the introduction of the Motronic MP 1.2 engine management system had led the way into capacity and, more significantly, compression ratio increases and with improved fuel power had been creeping towards 700b.h.p. by '85.

At Le Mans the organisers provided a mandatory fuel supply but elsewhere teams were able to bring their own supply. Group C fuel regulations were similar to those for Formula One and since '83 Formula One had shown the potential for the exploitation of such regulations. Essentially, the fuel chemist was able to brew a chemical compound which conformed to FISA's carefully worded definition of (maximum) 102 octane petrol yet which was far denser than pump petrol and which worked better in the turbo engine.

Indeed, the higher the turbo boost the more there was to be gained from the toluene based fuel used in mid Eighties Formula One engines - dubbed 'rocket fuel', it atomised extremely well at high pressure and was less heat intolerant that pump petrol, burning well and actually reducing the high pressure-intensified combustion chamber temperatures. Consequently, it upped the detonation threshold and was therefore effectively a higher octane fuel, though this did not register on the mandatory normal octane test, which was that designed to rate regular petrol. Rocket fuel produced power without effort and since it was far denser than pump petrol it allowed a car of mandatory maximum fuel tank volume to carry a greater weight of fuel.

Group C turbo cars were not as highly boosted as Formula One cars so an appropriate chemical brew was less 'radical'. However, the extra density afforded through use of toluene - a hydrocarbon not traditionally recognised as a power boosting additive and hence not illegal! - was clearly of benefit in any category restricted by volume of fuel carried. It was, however, not possible to brew a more potent or denser chemical fuel which could be considered 'legal' and which burned properly at atmospheric pressure and thus Jaguar could not exploit fuel chemistry. Walkinshaw had already started a campaign to restrict Group C to pump petrol but this would not bear fruit until 1987...

In the meantime, TWR sought to run 700b.h.p. race power on 102 octane pump petrol. Jaguar Engineering's 48 valve development engine was powerful and planned magnesium castings promised to save some of its excess weight. However, for a given power level it offered no significant fuel efficiency gain over Scott's excellent in-house two valve engine design.

Scott could already provide the power necessary to challenge Porsche from a slightly enlarged displacement but to run around 700 b.h.p. to the fuel ration the overweight chassis had to be made more efficient. The whole package had to be right (and TWR even had bespoke Kevlar-ply tyres under development at Fort Dunlop). As we have seen, the rolling road tunnel devised XJR-6 already had high downforce and the chassis specification was now starting to match this but there was clearly still a lot of scope to save weight.

Over the winter of '85/'86 much work went into trimming kilos from the over-engineered, rush-detailed prototype specification with as target the minimum 850kg. Of course, with the track experience of '85 and time on his side, Southgate was able to incorporate a number of significant detail improvements. He reflects that he was able, "to go right through the car and a much lighter and a much better XJR-6 came out". Overall efficiency was improved, while the major aerodynamic development was concerned with the production of a Le Mans specification.

Le Mans was the prime target for Jaguar and this year John Egan had been invited to start the race. TWR's approach to the event included 'borrowing' Redman and Haywood from Group 44 for their experience of the unique event. Aside from an specific aerodynamic package, TWR's preparation included rolling road endurance testing. This facility was available at Jaguar's now fully operational major new Engineering HQ at Whitley which already carried out rig testing for all parts of the corner assemblies - wheelbearings, hubs, uprights and so forth - and did brake pad bedding for TWR.

TWR's Kidlington headquarters contained Scott's expanding Engine Division and the developing race shop where the cars were now assembled from the parts supplied primarily by ACT, TCP, ART and Roni. All incoming parts were very carefully scrutinised by a well equipped inspection department and were numbered and lifed with such information stored on computer.

As we have noted, Jaguar had found a major sponsor for the '86 Group C programme in the form of Gallaher. This deal followed in the wake of Gallaher Chairman Peter Gilpin's move from rival

*Alastair McQueen joined the TWR team from Eddie Jordan Racing to look after the XJR-6 chassis.*

cigarette company Rothmans, sponsor of the works Porsche team. The proud British Racing Green consequently gave way to a ghastly 'Silk Cut' livery which was unveiled in January, before TWR was in a position to confirm its 1986 driver line up. Loss of Brundle had been a major blow. Walkinshaw eventually signed Derek Warwick and Eddie Cheever to head the effort, with Jean-Louis Schlesser and Gianfranco Brancatelli continuing to toil for the team.

In 1986 two cars would be run in a full World Sports Prototype Championship programme, with a third added for Le Mans. Southgate was still responsible for overall design control with new TWR recruit Alastair McQueen (ex-Eddie Jordan Racing) in charge of detail design and day to day engineering. McQueen race engineered the number

one car with Silman running the second entry. At Le Mans the cars would be run by McQueen, Eddie Hinckley and Paul Davis while Silman concentrated on overall Team Management.

Running three cars at Le Mans was a long standing Porsche tradition: experience told that, almost invariably, over the course of a 24 hour race one car would retire through mechanical misfortune, another through driver error, leaving one car which could, in theory, win - provided it didn't suffer major setback. Further, TWR would run three drivers per car. Three drivers were necessary in Silman's view given the level of concentration it would be necessary to sustain in the face of an intense struggle. And against Porsche the struggle would be nothing if not intense...

# The Real Thing

The '86 XJR-6 specification included a 6.5 litre engine, this displacement attained via a 94.0mm. bore with head and piston modified to suit. In round figures it offered 700b.h.p. at 7,300r.p.m., which was the regular race r.p.m. for '86, reducing to 7,000r.p.m. at Le Mans. The definitive valve springs were now available while to overcome the circlip problem Scott switched from conventional circlips to Teflon buttons, these free to rub against the liner. The Zytek-managed engine was otherwise essentially unchanged apart from on-going evolutionary changes to exhaust pipe diameters and lengths and to camshaft profiles, while mapping was a continual process.

Specific qualifying engines were not built as a matter of policy. Detail work by Engine Division had trimmed the weight of the V12 from 250kg. to 240kg. and henceforth the unit would be run in conjunction with a funnel intake which added somewhat to drag but made its contribution to the 40 - 50 b.h.p. winter power increase.

The chassis also ran a larger aluminium front radiator - from Behr - while retaining the oil radiator in the lefthand flank. In conjunction with the single water radiator was a revised nose inlet scoop which was now flanked by separate brake cooling inlets. That was indicative of the on going very subtle reprofiling of the overall shape in the ceaseless quest for improved lift and drag figures. The basic aerodynamic package was proving commendably adaptable, the car retaining its aerodynamic balance as it moved from slow to high speed circuits. Aerodynamically, the XJR-6 was not significantly modified for '86 - the emphasis of the winter update was on weight saving and efficiency, Southgate confirms.

A problem of a high splitter wear rate was solved through the permanent deployment of aluminium skins over aluminium honeycomb after wood, carbon and so forth had been rejected. The bodywork was lightened with thinner - and less costly - pre-preg glass/resin skins replacing the unnecessarily strong pre-preg carbon fibre over the Nomex honeycomb core.

The monocoque also lost weight - Southgate reckons perhaps 20lbs. - as TWR gained confidence with the structure. The basic concept remained unchanged the modification was of an evolutionary nature. McQueen was later to reflect: "Tony's original concept was spot on. At the time no one knew how strong, how rigid, how successful a carbon fibre composite sportscar tub would be. Confidence came with experience - in places the tub was found to be oversized or unnecessarily strong allowing substitution of a lighter carbon fibre/Kevlar weave".

A major change was a planned switch from aluminium plates to composite for the intermediate, two row front suspension bulkhead - bonding in the composite replacement produced a stronger front box structure. Throughout there was more use of aluminium rather than Nomex honeycomb to help save weight. The fuel tank area was extended, moving the seats forward 25mm. and this allowed installation of a single fuel cell: a simpler and lighter option which was easier to scavenge. The single cell was scavenged by four low pressure pumps, one set into each corner, which fed a central collector pot. Two high pressure pumps (for adequate capacity) then fed fuel from the pot inside the cell to the engine.

At the rear, the anti roll bar system was further modified to produce an extremely simple system. An extension forward from the leading leg of each upper wishbone essentially comprised the 'bar', with a pair of rod ends linking these two short arms. Each arm took the form of a blade that could be twisted to adjust bar stiffness. Meanwhile, at the front the conventional bar now took the form of a two inch diameter (1/4 inch wall) tube. McQueen confirms that the car had been going better with each increase in bar stiffness - the challenge was to avoid compromising driveability through making the front excessively stiff. Titanium rising rate springs had been evaluated but found unnecessary.

At the rear, a stay bar was added running from the spring/damper pick up at the end of the crossbeam down to the transaxle, cutting across the diffuser tunnel. The crossbeam had been controlled in a fore/aft direction through its rigid connections to the stiff tunnels but had been found to have its own spring rate. The stay bar was an unwelcome but necessary minor encroachment upon the tunnel space.

Brake development saw the caliper bolted directly into a suitably modified upright: improved detailing. More significantly, at the rear cooling was brought fully under control via periscope ducts projecting through the deck which fed down into the top of a hollowed out upright, while at the front the ducting now fed into the back of the upright. It was possible to take the feed from periscopes projecting through the nose if the front brakes were heavily stressed.

The transmission benefited as the Salisbury type

differential was modified by Roni to a TWR design (incorporating a few "special features"). The gearbox temperature gauge had proven an unnecessary distraction for the driver in the light of little temperature fluctuation and was replaced by a simple warning light. The '86 XJR-6 was one of the first race cars to employ the so called 'Intelligent Tachometer' developed by Stack Ltd of nearby Bicester and Maryland, USA. The Stack rev counter looked conventional enough but had an in-built micro processor which used quartz timing to measure engine speed and in addition to running a unique 'no waver' needle drive monitored engine revs and recorded the data for subsequent display on a portable printer.

Improved cockpit ventilation was now ensured via a feed from a NACA duct in the horizontal section of the driver's door with a flap to allow this to be shut off. This system followed a less effective attempt to duct air from under the radiator.

As planned, the net result of the various modifications was a more efficient car that was close to the weight limit. In the quest to save kilos even the rear air jack was removed: this was replaced by external air bags as the XJR-6 shaped up as a formidable Group C race car.

*By 1986 the XJR-6 was running a 6.5 litre displacement version of the Allan Scott developed Jaguar V12 engine. The air box was revised for a funnel feed.*

# Two Horse Race

Both Lancia and Porsche announced reduced works Group C programmes for 1986, Lancia to concentrate upon rallying, Porsche to concentrate upon research and development while leaving the title chase to its customer teams. However, unlike Lancia, Porsche would make a factory Le Mans effort - hoping to restore its honour...

Joest Racing had won Le Mans in 1984 and 1985 running the mechanical injection Typ 935/76 engine. Both mechanical and electronic Porsche engines could be produced in 2.65, 2.8, 3.0 and 3.2 litre displacements, the bigger displacement versions having been developed for German national sprint races. However, as we have noted, some customers had tried them in selected World Championship races - Joest was one known to have done so since '84. Converting a 2.65 litre to a 2.8 litre engine was simplicity itself: it was a case of buying the appropriate 70.4mm. stroke crankshaft and con rods to suit. To produce a 3.0 litre version it was then simply a case of taking the bore out to 95.0mm. and adding a set of new pistons and rings. However, there was no clear cut option for Group C racing, given the fuel ration.

Having run 2.65 litre Typ 935/82 engines throughout '84 and '85, the works Group C team started using the 3.0 litre version in '86, and began to phase in a fully watercooled derivative, the Typ 935/83. Other than for additional water jacketing to envelope the cylinder barrels, this was essentially to 935/82 specification. The factory also planned to campaign a 962C equipped with the experimental 'PDK' clutchless transmission first seen at Brands Hatch in '85. This had an electronically controlled double-clutch gearbox operated via buttons on the steering wheel which offered instant changes without so much as a lift of the throttle, let alone use of the clutch. That was, however, not in the interest of fuel saving and, worse, the clever PDK system added over 30kg., was as yet far from 100% dependable and punished driveshafts...

While Rothmans Porsche and Joest Racing continued to campaign conventional aluminium chassis, Brun Motorsport added the '84 constructed RLR aluminium honeycomb chassis to its stable and RLR built another ('Mark 2') honeycomb car, still with essentially standard aerodynamics. Other Porsche customer teams active in '86 included Kremer, Obermeier, Fitzpatrick and Cougar. Cougar was planning to run a Porsche chassis alongside its own Porsche-Cougar C12, the fastest car on the Mulsanne in 1985. However, the in house aluminium honeycomb chassis with aerodynamics designed specifically for Le Mans by Marcel Hubert (the engineer who shaped the '78 winning Renault) still lacked development mileage.

Aside from Jaguar, Porsche and sometimes Lancia, the only C1 contenders for the '86 title were Mercedes-Sauber and Aston Martin-Cheetah. Both Sauber and Cheetah had been seen in '85 - neither was a serious threat at this stage. Of the two the Sauber effort, assisted by Daimler Benz through the back door, was the one with long term potential. The Sauber car was well prepared and the its twin turbocharged 5.0 litre aluminium V8 promised much more performance than the normally aspirated 5.7 litre Aston Martin engine, particularly as it ran a Motronic engine management system...

A similar dark horse status was held by Nissan and Toyota, but these factory teams planned only to run Le Mans and Fuji. The '86 season was shaping up as a two horse race, albeit a classic one as Jaguar attempted to dethrone Porsche using very different technology...

A dark horse for Le Mans in 1986 - the turbocharged 5.0 litre Mercedes M117 engine was prepared by Heini Mader for the Sauber team. Daimler Benz lent back door support.

*The XJR-6 is prepared to do battle at Silverstone in the spring of '86. Note use of intermediate-length splitter here - a shorter version was run at Le Mans.*

# The Cat Growls

Off season '85/'86 testing revolved around the so called 'interim' car 385 - which had the third (and last) '85 specification monocoque but had been assembled late enough to benefit from the '86 specification in other areas. It was followed by two chassis (186 and 286) to full 'lightweight' specification. The test schedule included sun-seeking trips to Estoril in February and Paul Ricard in March, the latter circuit (with its high speed straight) the scene of a 24 hour run conducted in the strictest secrecy.

A novelty of the Estoril test was use of an AP Racing twin disc brake on all four corners of 385. The twin disc concept had been introduced by Girling in the early Seventies and the JW Automotive team had tried pioneering the Girling system on its Porsche 917K in practice for the 1971 Osterreichring 1000km. race. However, the system had not been adequately developed. AP Racing had revived the twin disc concept with the advent of carbon fibre reinforced carbon (CFRC, or carbon-carbon) discs.

AP Racing had done a deal with the American specialist Hitco - a division of the giant Armoc Steel corporation specialising in defence work - for the supply of the state-secret-manufacturing-process carbon-carbon material and had found the rival French Carbone Industrie (CI) aerospace concern's SEP company discs offering a marginally higher co-efficient of friction. AP Racing's Hitco discs were more stable, offering a more progressive rise in stopping power with increasing heat but CI discs gave additional bite. That was significant for the 1000b.h.p. Grand Prix cars of the mid Eighties, which put more heat into the disc and needed more stopping power than 500/600b.h.p. 'atmo' Formula One cars.

AP Racing's response was to try using two of the lightweight Hitco carbon-carbon discs together with a single caliper and this system was evaluated

The 1986 Silverstone 1000km. race was a historic occasion, Jaguar claiming its first World Championship sports car race victory since the Fifties. The winning car was running 7000r.p.m. for around 700b.h.p.

by Williams and Tyrrell. As a spin off from that project the company offered TWR a conventional, cast iron twin disc brake for the far heavier (850 rather than 550kg.) XJR-6. Two thin solid fully floating discs were squeezed by a single piston on the inside of the caliper. Conventional disc bells couldn't be fitted so the discs were run on a special dog drive.

The twin disc arrangement offered reduced pedal effort and less pedal travel. However, pad knock off was a problem until the single caliper was replaced by twin (balanced) calipers. That, of course, added weight and complexity while there was already a problem of cooling the two solid discs with no channel to blow air through. Problems mounted, then while Brancatelli was driving 385 one of the inner discs exploded and actually cut through the wheel and monocoque to land in the monocoque as the wheel flew off! The project was abandoned.

The Estoril and Ricard trials were run with the latest, revised construction Dunlop crossplies, as also supplied to the Porsche factory; as yet there was no sign of the 'Kevlar' tyres. The 24 hour run was conducted with 285 carrying conventional bodywork - the intention was to prove components rather than to evaluate Southgate's Le Mans aerodynamic package, which was still at the design stage. The test was not continued overnight and of the niggling problems which arose a good proportion were attributable to the artificial break in the proceedings. The test in fact was run to 23 hours 40 minutes during which the car covered

2376 miles. It was, says Silman, "a very valuable learning exercise".

The first race of the season was at Monza where the pair of '86 chassis (861 and 862) presented weighed in at 851 and 855kg., so successful had the winter diet programme been. The cars were running in low downforce trim with a short splitter (no longer than the nose) and a low set wing. The lighter, more powerful XJR-6s were, however, out-qualified by turbo power at Monza, as expected. When it counted, the cars were well in the running for the 365km. 'Super Sprint' - until a vapour lock problem then a c.v. joint failure put paid to the team's chances.

For Silverstone, air ducting to the fuel pumps together with a fuel cooler in the engine funnel guarded against vapour lock. Again turbo boost told in qualifying, Lancia running perhaps 1000b.h.p. to post a 1m 10.81s. pole time. Cheever managed a lap just a whisker over two seconds slower for third on the grid and it all came good in the first 1000km. race of the season. Only Lancia's single entry could find a race pace to match TWR and the pole car broke before it needed prove it had the fuel efficiency to sustain its pace.

*Autosport* called it, 'A Legend Reborn' but there was no false confidence for Le Mans. Rothmans Porsche had to some extent handicapped itself at Silverstone with the excess weight of the PDK transmission and would run two of three 24 hour entries with conventional transmission for an event in which the fuel allocation was up from 2210 to 2550 litres - back almost to the level of '82/'84. And

Porsche had the all-important experience of Le Mans.

TWR was fortunate that the ACO introduced a new test day this year, and this fell just four days after Silverstone. TWR, Rothmans Porsche and Nissan were the only major teams in attendance. As at Monza and Silverstone TWR had three chassis on hand, the third the rebuilt 385 which still carried about 20kg. excess. All three were fitted with Silverstone engines.

Car #51 - chassis 286 - remained in its Silverstone winning trim, apart from a shorter (Monza-type) splitter and a single element (low drag) rear wing while #52 - chassis 186 - had some of Southgate's new Le Mans package but only an 'interim' version of its low drag underwing. Car #53 - chassis 385 - had the full works. The Le Mans aerodynamic modifications were the fruit of four separate sessions at Imperial College and saw the full package offer significantly less downforce than the regular car as Southgate aimed for half the drag.

The complete Le Mans package included nose, underwing, tail and wing modifications. The Le Mans nose was to the regular form but lacked front wheel arch louvers and the regular lip across the front of the radiator exit. Underneath, adjustable size apertures were set in the radiator floor panel to bleed some of the high pressure air down to the underwing rather than letting it all exit up over the windscreen. Further, the low downforce nose was run with a short splitter and without front wheel infill plates.

The revised underwing had a marked lower downforce, lower drag characteristic with smaller diffuser tunnels very evident at the rear. The lower tunnels necessitated a forward bracing strut from the crossbeam since they no longer reached beam height. The tail was extended at the back, having a longer base but the same length rear deck. Clearly this was not streamlining in the traditional sense and it worked better with the new underwing and

the single element rear wing that was standard for Le Mans and was run lower in relation to the height of the rear deck. Indeed, the air saw the wing as an extension of the deck.

With the least drag #53 ran the fastest of the trio on the Mulsanne at 221m.p.h. That did not compare well to the '85 record 231m.p.h. clocking. In contrast car #51 porpoised and grounded along the straight as its high downforce multiplied with the square of its speed and it would not exceed 190m.p.h. However, it was significantly faster through the corners and over the entire lap it was just about as quick. Overall, though, it was harder work to drive to a good lap time and, more significantly, it consumed around 25% more fuel. And as a consequence of running its driveshafts at an "outrageous angle" on the Mulsanne (with the downforce pulling its transmission down) it fell by the wayside with c.v. joint failure.

Car #52 - the 'compromise' car - ran 214m.p.h. and managed a marginally quicker lap than #53, Cheever clocking the fastest time of the day in it. However, its aerodynamic loading was in the wrong place - the centre of pressure was too far forward which made it unstable on the Mulsanne and darty in response to steering wheel movements: stability is very much influenced by the location of the centre of pressure. The compromise car also burned more fuel than the low drag car. The test day confirmed what was required for an effective Le Mans package and the race cars would be prepared to the full low drag specification.

The circuit had been slightly revised at Mulsanne corner and there were no cars looking hard for an impressive lap time. Cheever clocked 3m. 21.89s. to head the timesheets while the best Porsche time was 3m. 23.40s. The other Jaguar times were 3m. 22.24s. for Schlesser in #53 and 3m. 25.27s. for Warwick in #51, the sprint car. Porsche was still concentrating on its PDK cars and this mysteriously cost it around 20m.p.h. on the Mulsanne, while Nissan was in all sorts of trouble...

Realistically, the Le Mans race favourite was going to be Porsche, as usual, while TWR got the feel of the event. There were no less than 14 Porsches in the field with the two conventional works cars, the PDK works car plus no less than 11 privately run machines headed by Joest's double-winning 956 chassis. Then there was the Porsche-Cougar, a lone Peugeot-WM, plus half a dozen other turbocharged outsiders: two cars each from Nissan, Toyota and Mercedes-Sauber. None of these could realistically hope to beat Porsche - could Jaguar?

TWR's preparation included 36 hours on the Jaguar rolling road and simulated running with the angled driveshafts at 10 degrees, twice the maximum run in practice. The cars presented for scrutineering were the three regular chassis - there was no spare - running fresh V12s fitted with Holset vibration dampers since the revs run on the Mulsanne were close to the natural frequency of the crankshaft where there was just a little torsional shake.

Aside from the aerodynamic package, the Le Mans chassis specification included brake and transmission modifications in response to the special demands of the event. The brake discs were changed from thinwall cross drilled to thickwall solid (of the same overall diameter and overall thickness) to provide more mass to absorb energy. This was in response to the effect of running cool on the Mulsanne straight then braking harshly for the Mulsanne corner. On the transmission side, the c.w.p. ratio was changed from 10/31 to 12/31 - regular gears were run, upped 1.2 by the Le Mans c.w.p. The effect was that of making top at Silverstone fourth at Le Mans.

*Jaguar tested its Le Mans aerodynamics at Silverstone in preparation for TWR's debut entry to the classic race. Note extended tail and low set single element wing with small endplates.*

*Jaguar publicity drawings emphasise tail and wing modifications for Le Mans '86 but incorrectly equip the XJR-6LM with a slow speed circuit splitter.*

Other Le Mans measures included a screen that was clamped in place rather than bonded in. The nose had twin headlights and the monocoque was fitted with extra wiring and switches for number lights, illuminated instruments and so forth. With special preparation for Le Mans all three cars registered around 870kg at scrutineering. The suspension, wheels and tyres were as per normal, with only spring and damper rates altered to suit the circuit.

Car #51 - again 286 - was driven by Cheever/Warwick/Schlesser, car #52 - again 186 - by Heyer and loaned Group 44 Le Mans veterans Redman and Haywood, car #53 - 385 - by Brancatelli/Win Percy/Armin Hahne. Qualifying saw only three cars dip under 3m. 20s., the pole sitting works 962C - without PDK - recording 3m. 15.99s. This was split from its conventional transmission sister car by the lead Joest 956 which ran the Mulsanne fastest of all at 232.4m.p.h. The three fast Porsches qualified with 3.0 litre engines. The quickest Jaguar, #51 in Cheever's capable hands, split the Brun team taking fifth place with a fine 3m 21.60s. lap while #52 posted 3m. 24.95s. in Heyer's hands for seventh on the grid.

Car #52 gave Haywood a moment when a rear Speedline shattered while #53 suffered a braking problem traced to hub bearing movement. Brancatelli qualified it 14th with 3m. 29.24s. It ran a best of 218m.p.h. while #52 recorded 221m.p.h. and the quickest Jaguar was the slowest at only 212m.p.h. Clearly, qualifying ahead of so many

turbo cars, good grip and handling compensated for the XJR-6's modest power and modest Mulsanne speed. But on 2550 litres, how would it race?

The cars were to be started by Warwick, Heyer and Brancatelli with driver changes planned after the first stint then after every other stint. There was a panic before the race got underway, fuel seen to be leaking from #52 as it was wheeled out for the preliminaries. It was necessary to drain all the fuel from the tank before the leak could be repaired with epoxy resin but there was time to complete the task.

From the rolling start Ludwig forged ahead in the Joest car but on the first lap Warwick was able to get up into a remarkable second spot and he held the Rothmans cars off for three memorable laps. The pattern which then became established was of three leading conventional Porsches chased by the PDK car and two of the three XJR-6s, #51 and #52 running strongly in the top six while #53 ran a more conservative pace, albeit still holding its own in the top 10. Indeed at the end of the first hour, after the first round of pit stops, the Jaguar placings were fourth, fifth and eighth.

Car #53 gained a place as the PDK Porsche spun out of contention but was lapped within three hours. The three hour mark found Heyer striving hard to keep #52 on the lead lap, a task that proved in vain. The car rolled to a halt at Indianapolis. The fuel calculation indicated 11 litres but the pumps

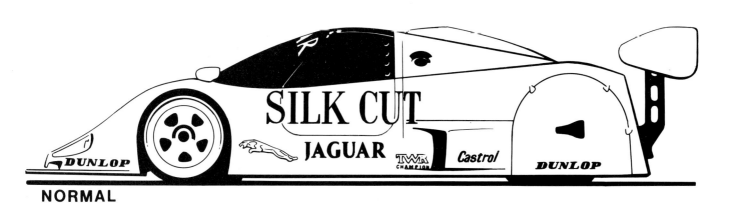

**NORMAL**

**LE MANS — low wing, longer tail**

SPENCER 86

were not delivering anything at all. A delegation was sent from the pit to shout advice, to no avail. After a couple of frustrating hours Heyer had to abandon the car. Its fuel cell was virtually dry, after all.

At the four hour mark the remaining TWR cars were fourth and fifth, one lap down on the three way lead battle and gradually slipping back. Were the leaders overstepping the fuel mark and gambling on an extended pace car period, or rain? It looked possible... TWR had not that strategic option - the XJR-6s had to run at essentially the same speed throughout, the race speed dictated by the revs chosen as compromise of fuel efficiency

A tyre blow out ended the chances of the Cheever/ Warwick/Schlesser XJR-6 at Le Mans in 1986. The strong driver line up helped ensure impressive speed prior to the misfortune.

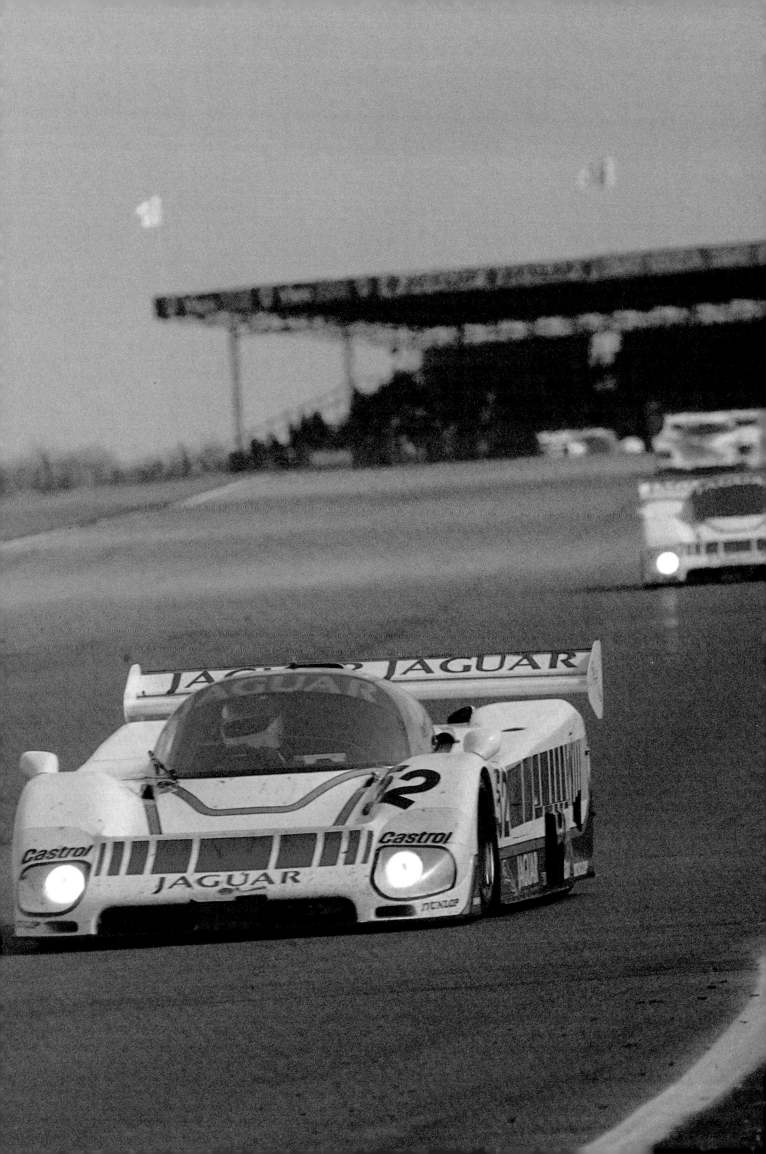

*The colour photographs on the preceding eight pages illustrate the XJR-6 on track in 1986. The photographs were taken at Silverstone (pages 89, 94-95 and 96), Le Mans (pages 90-91) and Spa Francorchamps.*

*TWR had speed but an understandable lack of stamina at Le Mans in '86. Car #52 ran out of fuel while car #51 suffered terminal damage following a tyre blow out. Car #53 suffered c.v. joint failure.*

and reliability. Six hours found the Jaguar representatives two and three laps down, but still fourth and fifth. Only the Brun team looked threatening. And there had never been more than two marques in this race: Porsche and Jaguar...

Jaguar hopes took another tumble just before 11.00pm when Schlesser came in after one lap complaining of dim headlights. The alternator was overheating and compressed air had to be used to cool it. Then the starter motor needed coaxing with a little cold water. The tail having been lifted to employ that fix, a marshal insisted that the engine be restarted with the body in place. That necessitated a battery change and with a total of 21 minutes - half a dozen laps - lost #51 fell to ninth position.

Car #53 continued to run well until 1.47am. when a c.v. joint broke giving Percy a dramatic moment as the car slewed sideways. He was unable to get it back to the pits. Two down...

The race took a tragic twist at 3.15am. when

Gartner's Kremer Porsche crashed, taking the life of its driver. During a two and a half hour pace car stint the Ludwig Porsche overheated its engine while the surviving Porsches won a significant fuel bonus. Just before the Gartner accident one of the leading works cars had spun off on oil, and the race got underway again with the #51 and one of the Brun cars vying for second place eight laps in arrears. Jaguar's hope got the upper hand and kept pace with the leader, but the leader had no cause to hurry at this stage, and had fuel to spare...

Second place would have been a worthy result but just before 8.30am. it all went wrong for #51. The right rear tyre burst as Schlesser left the kink, heading up to the brow before Mulsanne corner. Unlike Porsche, TWR did not yet have tyre pressure sensing device. Thankfully, the beads stayed in place but tread flew off and damaged the bodywork. The car stayed on the track and Schlesser was able to nurse it home. Alas, aside from a broken underbody and tail and ripped

brake lines, the suspension had been wrecked and the bellhousing had suffered a crack. That made a repair impractical.

Following the Le Mans experience, cooling air was ducted to the starter and alternator from the existing air vent in the right hand flank of the tail. More than one starter motor had gone into 'meltdown' during the course of the race! The first race after the French classic was a 182km. sprint at the Norisring, a track with fast sections punctuated by tight hairpins. Here watercooling for the brakes was toyed with. Ludwig's Joest Porsche won, narrowly defeating Cheever while Warwick came in third. Then it was back to the business of 1000km. racing, with events at Brands Hatch, Jerez, the new Nurburgring, Spa Francorchamps and Fuji concluding the season.

Jaguar enthusiasts looking for a repeat of Silverstone were disappointed: the only win was in a one-off German Supercup race at the Nurburgring towards the end of the season. At Brands Hatch delays including a loose wheelbearing and a blocked fuel filter saw fourth and sixth placings. At Jerez three cars were run and all three spun off at the first corner in an incident prompted by Warwick. Warwick/ Lammers recovered to third; the others retired. At the 'Ring the Warwick/Lammers pairing was heading for victory when a rare engine failure struck, at Spa Warwick was a very close second to Boutsen's Brun Porsche after both cars spluttered out of fuel...

In spite of all that drama second at Fuji would have been good enough to have given TWR and Warwick world titles. He and Lammers finished third thanks to a broken ignition wire. The story of the season - small, often niggling problems stopped sustained success. Nevertheless, the XJR-6 was already a technical success: it had raised the bench mark for 1000km. pace in its first full season.

*The XJR-6 failed to add to its Silverstone victory over the balance of the '86 season. Note periscope front brake scoops fitted for circuits heavy on braking, such as here at Brands Hatch.*

# Seeking Stamina

In 1986 TWR had learned how to fine tune its electronically managed engine and its sophisticated chassis from circuit to circuit for the best fuel efficiency and for 1987 Scott was able to increase the engine displacement to 7.0 litres, primarily seeking additional torque. With more torque there would be less gear changing, the car pulling a higher gear and thus running less revs to the benefit of fuel economy. And while TWR was dialling in additional performance, the turbo runners were having to adapt to mandatory pump petrol...

1987 looked promising for Jaguar hopes, particularly as the XJR-6 had demonstrated such highly competitive speed throughout 1986. Over the offseason TWR went through the car with a fine toothcomb aiming to eradicate any possible source of weakness and the duly revised machine was given a new designation, XJR-8. It was, at last, to have the promised Kevlar-based crossplies as Dunlop rose to the challenge of the superior Michelin radials run by Brun over the latter half of '86.

With continuing Gallaher backing TWR was able to sign four very strong drivers for its regular two car entry: Cheever, Lammers, Watson and Raul Boesel, an Indy Car driver who had flirted with Formula One somewhat prematurely but had come back to Europe to impress TWR during its pre-season testing. Nielsen would replace Cheever when Arrows Formula One commitments took priority and various drivers were under consideration to help make up the three car Le Mans team. The regular race engineers this season were McQueen and Hinckley, with Ken Page running the third Le Mans car.

This time around with some experience to fall back upon, there was a real chance of 24 hour glory and at Kidlington a task force had been created to develop a car specifically for the race. Under the direction of Silman, Southgate and McQueen, since October '86 mechanic Clive Parker and two assistants had been permanently assigned to the '87 Le Mans project. Southgate spent a lot more time at Imperial College looking specifically at the demands of Le Mans and the prototype 'XJR-8LM' was running in February '87. The bespoke Le Mans package embraced significant mechanical as well as aerodynamic alterations - this really was a no-compromise effort...

Engine Division took
its V12 power plant
to 7.0 litres for
1987. The main
gain was additional
torque. The
enlarged unit was
matched to a
revised chassis
codenamed XJR-8.

# Many Changes

TWR announced that "64 significant changes" turned an XJR-6 into an XJR-8, in addition to which there was the important engine modification as Engine Division went from 6.5 to 7.0litres. The larger displacement was straightforward to enough attain, through installation of an 84.0mm. crankshaft, 94.0 x 84.0mm. providing a total displacement of 6995.3cc. Otherwise the engine was fundamentally unaltered and it was 'tuned' to give only an extra 15 - 20b.h.p. top end power while pumping out an extra 45b.h.p. at 5,500r.p.m. Maximum torque went from 570lb.ft. to 605lb.ft. at 5,250r.p.m. - that was the real gain. And Scott had been able to achieve a commendably flat torque curve - from 4,750r.p.m. to 6,250r.p.m. it was within 3% of a straight line.

The long stroke TWR V12 punished new Kevlar ply tyres supplied to both TWR and Porsche and first tested by TWR on an XJR-6 at Sebring in December '86. It had taken a long while for Dunlop to find a means to produce the new tyres requested by TWR. Unlike conventional crossplies, they didn't grow at speed offering the dimensional stability previously only associated with radials. Southgate says that 5mm. to 6mm. was the maximum dimensional change experienced with the Kevlar plies. Such stability is of particular importance for a ground effect car since ride height needs to stay as consistent as possible for maximum performance from the underwing.

The new tyres were monitored by a new tyre temperature sensor jointly developed by TWR and Zytek in the light of the unavailability of the Porsche/Bosch pressure sensor. The Porsche/Bosch sensor read the pressure within a specially modified rim, and Bosch was apparently unready to produce in quantity sufficient to service both Porsche and TWR. The TWR sensor was based on an infra red heat scanner which read the temperature on the surface of the tyre. The scanner was an expensive optical device (applied in a variety of fields) which resembled a video camera lens and was positioned only fractionally away from the tyre surface. The so called 'Heat Spy' indicated the condition of the tyre with steadily rising temperature a symptom of dangerous pressure loss which was highlighted by a red warning light on the dashboard. The driver could also call up temperature readings for each tyre on a combined Zytek digital fuel consumption/tyre temperature read out.

The Heat Spy system logged tyre temperature data on a continual time basis, providing very valuable information for the Dunlop technicians. For the driver, the tyre temperature readings were particularly useful in qualifying, allowing him to 'lean' on his tyres while making sure they didn't get too hot and consequently go off. With the new Kevlar based tyres Dunlop requested a wider, 13" front rim for sidewall stability. The wheels were switched from Speedlines to Dymags, still one piece magnesium but diecast rather than sand cast. Dymag, which had not previously produced a 19" diameter rear rim, boasted of a stronger, more durable product and subsequent crack tests would validate this claim.

A major XJR-8 chassis development was a carbon fibre front anti roll bar. Used in conjunction with new tub mountings and revised uprights (to which it was directly connected), this was, says Southgate, "90% efficient" whereas the previous 2" steel tube had been at best "60% efficient". The carbon fibre bar took the form of a hollow tube of which the stiffness was determined by the direction of the fibres and the lay up employed. It was half the weight of the steel bar yet could offer twice the stiffness. In comparison, Southgate remarks that the steel bar was "like a girder". Three types were produced - soft, intermediate, hard - rated via rig tests, and for a half a ton load a mere half inch deflection indicated a soft bar.

The higher efficiency carbon fibre bar was an important step in control of the front end, given the weight transfer problems posed by the heavy, high centre of gravity V12. Another step was a higher roll centre - now very high by Formula One standards - provided by modified suspension geometry. "It was another attempt at the centre of gravity problem", Southgate admits, "and made the car easier to handle".

The revised front anti roll bar mounting allowed improved front brake ducting. A new 'shell duct' took air from the nose inlet flanking the radiator inlet and split it to feed separately the disc through the rear of the upright and the caliper. The caliper itself was an improved AP Racing model with differential bores to avoid taper wear. Another item of improved running gear was the driveshaft, which now came from Unicardan in Germany as a sealed assembly complete with conventional c.v. joints. The shaft itself had rolled splines and was claimed to be "bullet proof". The assembly was run in on a Jaguar Engineering rig - in both directions and at varying running angles - and any heating of the joints was outside acceptable tolerance.

*Rear end of the 7.0 litre V12 engine with AP Racing triple plate clutch mated to flywheel cum starter ring. The starter motor is still located at the front of the engine.*

In its regular 'sprint' trim the XJR-8 essentially retained the very effective aerodynamics of the standard '86 car with detail changes reflecting the on going development programme: larger rear wing end plates were indicative of this evolutionary process. However, an important step was a revised underwing featuring longer, more gently inclined tunnels that started underneath the monocoque. This demanded a revised tub with appropriate floor indents. Slot-in panels offered a choice of tunnel start. With the indent Southgate could use every last millimetre aft of the 800mm. long flat surface area.

The revised tub was fitted with a NACA-style

cockpit roof indent to channel air into the airbox, this modification avoiding the need for a pronounced funnel-type collector. The roof indent demanded an extra shaped panel which had to be bonded into the composite tub structure. Further complexity in the cockpit area was added by new front hinged doors that offered better water sealing. The doors had needed re-engineering since they had become too heavy and the gullwing pattern had been abandoned with an eye to IMSA GTP regulations.

By this stage the monocoque employed aluminium honeycomb throughout and the XJR-8 featured rubbing strips running parallel to the horizontal side skirts just inside its floor area, and more convenient seat back rather than engine bay access to the fuel tank. The fuel system was revised again since the weight of the four scavenge pumps had tended to deform the fuel cell. Instead, four lightweight pick ups were serviced by two pumps, one each side of the central collector pot.

The twin high pressure pumps between the collector pot and the engine were relocated in a more easily accessible side box location, under a hatch in the passenger sill. In this cavity the pumps and associated filter were mounted on a quick release board which, having snap-off unions, could be changed in 30 seconds. The battery was similarly secured by quick-release catches in a cavity in the right hand sill for a similar 30 second switch. Further, mechanics working on these items would not be in the way of others working in the engine bay. Moving the pumps and battery was part of a general re-working of the engine bay aimed at ease of service, potentially of great benefit at Le Mans. After Heyer's unhappy experience at Le Mans in '86, there was now a reserve fuel tank.

Weight had been saved in a number of areas, including the bodywork. This had been lightened by switching from glass to Kevlar pre-preg for the skins, with carbon fibre reinforcement in places. The tunnels were now carbon fibre over aluminium honeycomb, which was thinner to save weight. Typical of various detail weight savings was the rear anti roll bar: this now employed only one blade (on the righthand side) since the finer adjustment offered by the two blade system could conveniently be dispensed with. The single blade and rocker system was simpler, and it was lighter since like the front bar it was in carbon fibre. With less weight, TWR was able to reinstate the on board air jacks, while the car then still required ballast. Driver cooling was improved via a new central nose air intake and an exit that opened into the new cockpit roof indent. A good through flow was important to proper functioning of the cockpit ventilation system, which set dashboard vents pointing at the driver's chest.

Three new XJR-8 monocoques were produced while the three chassis built during '86 were recycled. Chassis 186 became the prototype XJR-8LM which was finished in early February while 286 was also converted to 8LM specification, this job finished in April. Meanwhile, 386 had been converted to XJR-8 sprint specification to act as the team spare alongside 187 and 287 with 387 earmarked as the third 8LM chassis.

The Le Mans version retained the standard monocoque but had an angled drivetrain. The engine and transaxle assembly was tilted up at 2.5 degrees from the horizontal so that the c.w.p. was set higher and consequently the driveshafts did not have to work through an angle. Failure of an inner c.v. joint at Le Mans in '86 had been a direct consequence of the angle through which the halfshafts operated. The tilted drivetrain required modified engine mounts and certain rear suspension alterations. It raised the centre of gravity since half the weight of the engine plus the weight of the transaxle was raised approximately 50mm.

Further, strengthened halfshafts and bigger c.v. joints were fitted while to improve c.v. joint lubrication a special grease was developed by Castrol. The Le Mans driveshafts, of regular diameter, were hollow and of spring steel which allowed them to wind up and thus absorb shock loading. The larger c.v. joints could only be fitted in view of the use of a spool (a solid link between the drive shafts) - a differential blocked the space needed for their accommodation.

A spool was known to create understeer when attacking fast corners: it couldn't be run at Spa Francorchamps, for example. With a spool it was only possible to turn into a corner off the power. As all corners required that technique at Le Mans it was possible to run a spool and the advantage was of being able to return to the pits should a c.v. joint fail.

Other alterations to the running gear for the 8LM followed those introduced for Le Mans in '86, such as thickwall undrilled discs, clamped in screen, altered c.w.p. ratio and so forth. This year the starter was fitted via a quick release kit and the alternator was larger.

The '87 Le Mans aerodynamic package was similar in essence to that run in '86 and the tunnels still commenced behind the tub. However, the tail was shorter and was not fitted with rear wheel covers. The lack of wheel covers was a concession to the mechanics, who were further assisted by the shorter, less obtrusive tail which had the additional advantage of causing less rear light vibration.

Loss of the wheel covers cost some downforce but overall downforce was up compared to '86 while drag was no less than 13% lower. The improvement came from modification to the underwing and rear wing as well as the new shorter tail, with a subtly revised relationship between those items. Although the tail was shorter, the low set wing worked as an extension of the tail as well as a diffuser activator - the air saw the '87 car as a long tail design in spite of its outward appearance. With the '87 package the transmission cooler was relocated in the righthand flank of the tail.

# Pure Water

As we have seen, the increasing competition provided by Jaguar had led Porsche to develop a fully water cooled 3.0 litre engine, the Typ 935/83. This was employed by the factory team in '87 and was run with a new Bosch injector that offered a revised spray pattern for better atomisation given the strictly pump petrol. For the Typ 935/83, maximum r.p.m. was up from 8,400 to 8,800 r.p.m. At 2.4 bar absolute race pressure power went over 700 b.h.p. (rivalling that of the '86 3.2 litre two valve IMSA engine which had run on high octane fuel). The fully water cooled engine was, however, only for the use of the works team which continued to employ the regular 962C chassis, sometimes with a now 15kg. lighter and a more reliable PDK transmission. In Langheck guise 16" rear wheels

were fitted for a lower arch bulge which improved the airflow to the rear wing.

Among the privateer army, there was a proliferation of honeycomb replacement monocoques, some ordered from John Thompson. There was also a certain degree of experimentation on the aerodynamic front. Britten Lloyd Racing produced an entirely new aerodynamic package for its 962C as the Jaguar and Porsche factory teams set higher performance standards.

This season Lancia was missing but the Mercedes-Sauber challenge was growing and Nissan and Toyota were developing more effective Le Mans cars, with improved V8 turbo and in line four turbo power plants, respectively, as was Cougar which continued to employ Porsche power.

*Toyota's 3S-GT engine offered up to 750 b.h.p. in qualifying.*

# A Steamroller, but not for 24 Hours...

The prototype XJR-8LM was one of three cars taken to Paul Ricard in February '87 for a major five day test, the other machines being an XJR-8 in sprint trim (debuted earlier, at Donington) plus an XJR-6 in similar guise to act as a 'reference point'. The XJR-8 demonstrated a useful performance gain while the Le Mans version ran through 27 hours (again stopping overnight) suffering nothing more serious than a fractured exhaust bracket. However, with its higher centre of gravity the Le Mans car was proving more tricky to handle - to the driver it felt as if the top heavy engine was trying to come over his shoulder!

The season commenced with the first TWR pole at the slow Jarama circuit followed by wins at Jarama (a 360km. sprint race), Jerez and Monza. Rothmans Porsche looked to have a slight advantage in the Jerez race before it hit problems but the wins at Jarama and Monza were emphatic

*The 7.0 litre XJR-8 got mileage under its belt at Paul Ricard early in '87, as pictured below. Right, the car is seen disassembled at Monza during preparations for the Italian 1000km. race. The NACA scoop in the roof identifies an XJR-8 specification monocoque.*

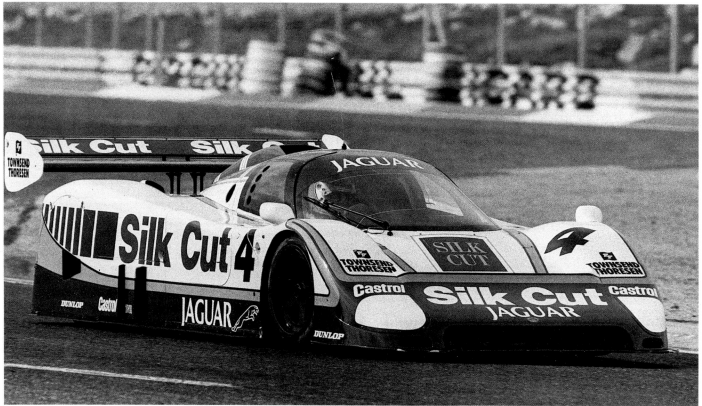

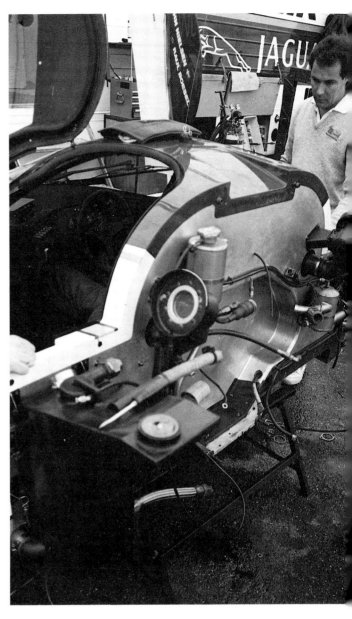

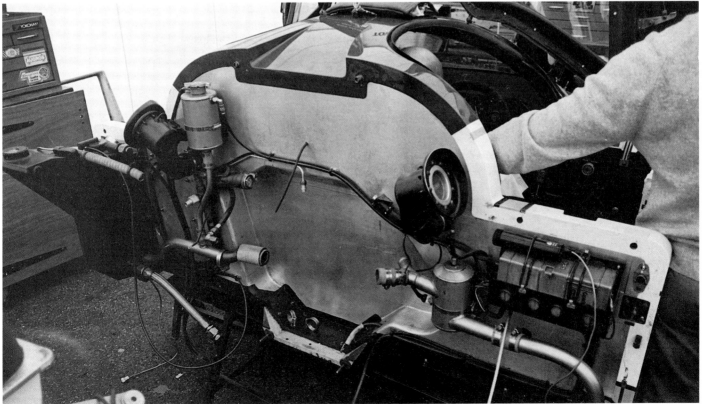

*Overhead shots of the XJR-8 in action at Monza (left/above/right) show the clean lines of the '87 model. At Monza TWR achieved its first hat trick of World Championship race wins, then it added a fourth in a row at Silverstone, below.*

enough. Meanwhile, the prototype 8LM had undergone further tests at Donington, Snetterton and Silverstone as a result of which some Kevlar panels had been thickened to minimise stone damage. On all cars the carbon fibre rear anti roll bar had been replaced by a metal item since the resin had started to break down faced with the heat of the engine bay.

The 8LM was entered as a third car for the Silverstone 1000km. in early May. "It was good experience to run a car in Le Mans specification in race conditions", says Silman, "and forced us to operate a three car team again, which was valuable experience from the organisational point of view".

The 8LM was run by Ken Page in full Le Mans trim with Brundle - now a Zakspeed driver and rejoining TWR specifically for Le Mans - and Nielsen its drivers. With extra weight (around 880kg.), reduced downforce, and more difficult handling the 8LM was not expected to match the pace of the sprint cars. It lapped less than three seconds slower en route to 10th on the grid, exceeding 200m.p.h. on the straights.

Silverstone was notable for the emergence of the Mercedes-Sauber as a competitive force with an improved C9 chassis design. The new C9 shared the front row with the fastest Rothmans Porsche as the turbo cars again boosted ahead of Jaguar on the grid. However, the Swiss built newcomer lacked development and the race was another Jaguar tour de force - and further proof that TWR had found reliability in '87, the sprint cars finishing first and second.

The 8LM was spun by Nielsen. As it was going backwards at around 100m.p.h. his foot slipped off the clutch and the timing chain jumped a couple of teeth as the engine was jerked violently to a halt. The car restarted and ran 20 minutes with the valves hitting the pistons before its abused V12 cried enough.

One week later chassis 186 was joined by 286 and

newly completed 387, its sister LM cars, for the Le Mans test day which this year was attended by ten C1 teams including Rothmans Porsche, the Joest and Kremer Porsche teams, Nissan, Toyota and Cougar. A novelty was a chicane at the Dunlop curve while the section from Indianapolis to the Porsche curves had been re-surfaced.

The Porsche factory had only a single car - in Langheck trim - on hand and this ran a strangely slow 215m.p.h. on the Mulsanne. Jaguar recorded a 225m.p.h. best while the latest Porsche-Cougar topped that with 229m.p.h., fastest of the day. However, Jaguar was quickest over the lap, Boesel clocking 3m 24.38s. compared to 3m.25.04s. for Wollek in the works Porsche and 3m.27.16s. for Raphanel in the Cougar. Given that Porsche was temporarily lacking Mulsanne *vitesse*, the '87 specification 962C could be expected to be a formidable opponent on the day. The times were not comparable with those of '86 due to the new chicane.

This year's running of the 24 hour classic brought forth 13 962Cs including three factory cars, two from Joest, two from Kremer and Britten Lloyd Racing's new 'trick' version. However, the evidence of the season so far suggested that the privateers, running Typ 935/82 engines, had lost competitive pace. Other possible threats included two Mercedes-Sauber C9s and two cars apiece from the Nissan and Toyota factories, the former backed

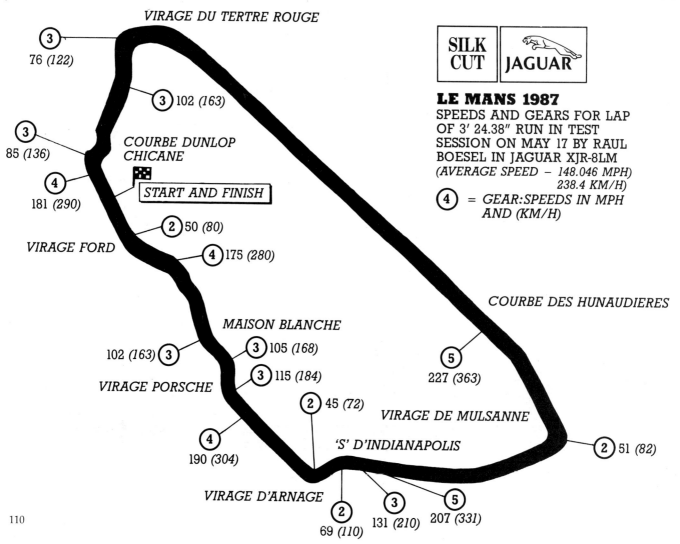

SILK CUT JAGUAR

**LE MANS 1987**
SPEEDS AND GEARS FOR LAP OF 3' 24.38" RUN IN TEST SESSION ON MAY 17 BY RAUL BOESEL IN JAGUAR XJR-8LM
(AVERAGE SPEED – 148.046 MPH) 238.4 KM/H)
④ = GEAR:SPEEDS IN MPH AND (KM/H)

VIRAGE DU TERTRE ROUGE

③ 76 (122)

③ 102 (163)

③ 85 (136)

COURBE DUNLOP CHICANE

④ 181 (290)

START AND FINISH

② 50 (80)

VIRAGE FORD

④ 175 (280)

COURBE DES HUNAUDIERES

MAISON BLANCHE

③ 105 (168)

102 (163) ③

③ 115 (184)

VIRAGE PORSCHE

② 45 (72)

⑤ 227 (363)

VIRAGE DE MULSANNE

'S' D'INDIANAPOLIS

② 51 (82)

④ 190 (304)

VIRAGE D'ARNAGE

② 69 (110)

③ 131 (210)

⑤ 207 (331)

up by two Electramotive V6 engined cars. And then there was the WM team, with a 'special' aimed specifically at 400k.p.h. (250m.p.h.) on the Mulsanne.

Rothmans Porsche was without a spare car following a late testing shunt and lost another chassis in qualifying. Nevertheless, the depleted two car team comfortably wrapped up the front row of the grid boasting a high boost pole time of 3m. 21.09s. from Wollek. In contrast, the quickest private 962C, one of the Joest cars, managed only 3m. 27.53s. Which left the second, third and fourth rows of the grid to Jaguar, Cougar and Sauber - in that order. The Cougar lacked race mileage and the Sauber C9 was known to be weak in the transmission department: this race was Weissach versus Kidlington.

The quickest qualifying Jaguar driver was Cheever who posted 3m. 24.36s. for third spot, and all three cars qualified at under 3m. 25s. Cheever, Brundle and Lammers made the times, Lammers slowest at 3m. 24.98s. but running race tyres. Strangely, the fastest speed recorded on the Mulsanne was 220m.p.h., all three cars running around that mark. However, the centre of pressure was further back this year and the cars were less darty on the long 'chute', if less comfortable to handle elsewhere thanks to the angled drivetrain. The driver pairings were Cheever and Boesel in #4 - chassis 387 - Lammers/Watson in #5 - chassis 286

The XJR-8LM ran at Paul Ricard, Silverstone (left) and Le Mans (lower left) prior to the 1987 24 hour race. The Jaguar publicity drawings highlight obvious bodywork modifications, again with incorrect spoiler length for the LM version. Overleaf, on page 112, the car is seen in action during the actual race.

**SPRINT**

**LE MANS**

The colour photographs on the eight preceding pages illustrate the XJR-8 on track in 1987. The photographs were all taken at Le Mans, aside from that opposite which was taken at Brands Hatch. The carbon fibre front anti roll bar is clearly visible in the photograph on page 113.

- and Brundle/Nielsen in #6 - chassis 186 - with Percy listed as a reserve driver for #5, Hahne for #6.

The opening stages of the race were confused by a damp track - Cheever and Lammers started on wets and stopped on lap two for slicks while Brundle continued with intermediates - and by sudden retirements of three of the quickest Porsches. Both Joest cars and one Kremer car failed. These were followed soon after the one hour mark by Mass' works car. Meantime, EPROMs had been switched in panic. Almost certainly the problem was the race day fuel supply. Subsequent laboratory tests by Porsche and WM - which also suffered - suggested an octane rating so low that it was right on the borderline of FISA regulations.

Thankfully the turbocharged ranks hadn't been completely decimated - Jaguar wouldn't have wanted to have won by default - but as the race settled down there were only five cars in strong contention and all but two represented Jaguar. The Stuck/Bell works Porsche led #6, the Britten Lloyd Racing 962C, #4 and #5 with the Saubers already falling back and soon to be lapped along with the rabbits. Of course, it only takes two cars to make a race and a superb duel for the lead was the highlight of Saturday evening, Bell and Nielsen sometimes running side by side down the Mulsanne as they jousted in Formula Three fashion.

TWR suspected that the 962C, which must have lost fuel efficiency through its change of chip, was overstepping the mark, Porsche (typically) gambling on bad weather or pace car consumption gains to come. And the first pace car incident wasn't long in coming, breaking up the absorbing battle for the lead. Thereafter, as daylight turned to dusk, Brundle took #6 a minute head of the works Porsche while the pursuing Jaguars, now ahead of the British 962C special, fell a lap behind. Car #4 subsequently lost a further lap due to a broken throttle cable and into the night, as showers fell, was chasing the Britten Lloyd machine for fourth place.

Stuck, a master of the wet, used the conditions to move back into the lead, then at 11.30pm. the pace car came out again: the Britten Lloyd 962C had mysteriously caught fire, burning out at the trackside thankfully without injury to driver James Weaver. Midnight found the race still under the ensuing pace car situation, now clearly one Porsche versus three Jaguars with the last Jaguar - #4 - just two laps adrift.

On a clear track again, Brundle/Nielsen were content to shadow Stuck/Bell, taking heart from the fact that the XJR-8 was burning less fuel than the Porsche it was tracking. At 1.30am. Lammers arrived in the pits without the tail of #5 - unnoticed by him it had come adrift. Repairs to the tail mounts dropped the car back onto the same lap as #4. Later Percy took a relief stint in #5 and there was a further delay since he brushed the brake pedal while the pads were being changed. As a

result the pistons fell out of the caliper and there was no option but to change the hot unit.

Out on the track, there was more misfortune in store for Winston Percy. Towards 3.00am., early in this first stint, he suffered every Le Mans driver's dread: tyre failure at the kink. His tyre pressure sensors had become inoperative, the Heat Spy glasses obscured by muck and grime thrown off the damp track. Unknowingly, Percy had incurred a slow puncture. The tyre had been kept up by centrifugal force on the Mulsanne...until it took side loading in the flat out kink.

The left rear was the culprit. Its collapse pitched the car into the new three tier barrier at full tilt, over 200m.p.h. It flew through the air and rolled sideways on the track, Percy's helmet scraping the surface as the doors had been lost. But though the outer panels of the monocoque got deformed the inner panels stayed intact. Not a drop of fuel - and the tank was well over half full - spilled and the so called 'survival cell' proved just that. Percy was able to walk away. Thankfully, the accident had been a long one, providing plenty of time in which to dissipate the energy of the crashing car. Short high speed shunts are the most deadly. Nevertheless, it cannot be denied that TWR's monocoque had done a superb job of protection for its shaken but uninjured occupant.

As a precaution the Kevlar tyres on the other cars were changed for conventional older tyres but after a couple of hours - mainly run under the pace car - regular '87 rubber was reinstated. The accident had been attributed to a puncture caused by track debris.

As the race resumed after the half distance mark the order was Porsche - one lap - #6 - one lap - #4 - ten laps - the rest... Soon it was light again, the early rays revealing an unusually close Sunday race. However, the long (one and three quarter hour) pace car period following Percy's accident had clearly strengthened Porsche's hand.

At 6.45am. Boesel spun at Arnage and damaged the nose of #4, which fell four laps behind, then as that was being sorted out #6 made its first unscheduled stop. It was a vibration problem: two stops switching tyres cost all but another lap to the leader. Then, with two thirds of the race run, the car overheated. It was pushed away victim of a cracked cylinder head. It has to be appreciated that TWR was working from production car heads, cast on the production car line. Head casting failure was nevertheless previously unknown.

Meanwhile #4 had run into gearbox trouble. A screw retaining the oil pump had loosened and fallen out, hitting a gear: chaos! The case was punctured, necessitating an araldite patch as well as replacement of its internals. The repairs dropped it to third, now hopelessly out of contention for victory other than by default, though second place was regained without too much trouble.

Soon after 10.00am. Boesel stopped on the Mulsanne. Thankfully he was able to diagnose a broken ignition trigger wire and switch to the back

up trigger. However, he failed to secure the tail properly and it flew off, extending the delay. Then an hour later Cheever stopped on the Mulsanne, having lost fuel pressure. He was able to coax the car back to the pits for a change of pumps but it was now 24 laps behind. And that became 30 laps with a late change of upright to cure severe vibration. The upshot was fifth place.

The mechanics who did so much to bring the car home - Parker with Jeff Wilson, Alva Claxton, Chris Tuckey and Tim Strudwick - were rightly awarded the first 'Prix ESCRA', a trophy for the crew judged to have made the greatest contribution to the success of their car.

After Le Mans the ECU became programmable directly from a portable micro rather than via a plug-in EPROM, Zytek ever striving to make its system more "user friendly". Two weeks on and the action switched to contrasting Norisring sprint race (for which a new chassis was phased in). This year the event was run as two heats for a total of 360km. Sadly, the factory Porsche team had announced a withdrawal from the World Sports-Prototype Championship. However, here it fielded its regular Supercup car for Stuck and Bell.

In the first heat Cheever suffered fuel pump failure and lost seven laps while, having taken the lead, Lammers suffered a broken differential. Nevertheless, Cheever's partner Boesel was awarded the second heat after the winning Joest car had been disqualified for an infringement of the technical regulations. That added up to fourth overall - and the second and last defeat of '87...

Aside, that is, from a one-off Hockenheim Supercup race late in the season. An XJR-8 for Boesel was crushed by the Porsche opposition at this fast circuit. The defeat - in a pure sprint race - highlighted the fact that the XJR-8 had exceptional downforce at the cost of high drag, a consideration which helped influence the design of forthcoming XJR-9.

On the title trail, Brands Hatch, the 'Ring, Spa Francorchamps and Fuji witnessed four wins in a row against the Porsche privateers (some loaned Typ 935/83 engines) and the improving Sauber team for a total of eight '87 victories. The overall tally read 16 finishes from 23 starts, including Le Mans: a commendable achievement. Boesel won the Driver's crown and TWR scored almost double the points of its nearest rival for the Teams title.

After Le Mans (previous double page spread) the XJR-8 resumed its winning ways at Brands Hatch (below) and thereafter there was no stopping the victory machine. Sadly Porsche had now withdrawn its factory team from 1000km. race participation but the Mercedes-Sauber challenge was starting to shape up as serious opposition.

88

# Two More Targets

Since 1985 Jaguar had ambitiously held three targets for its Sports-Prototype racing involvement: Le Mans, the World Sports-Prototype and the IMSA Camel GT Championships. And now TWR had lifted the World crown it was to aim for both the coveted Le Mans victory and the elusive IMSA title. The decision to switch the IMSA programme had been taken early in '87 and by mid season Guy Edwards had found a sponsor for TWR's '88 American bid in the form of the Castrol importer.

Meanwhile, Scott was busy developing his 7.0 litre engine to run on high octane fuel and Southgate was drawing a suitably modified, 900kg. chassis to run to GTP regulations which called for a 120 litre fuel tank and equal diameter front and rear wheel rims. The effort at Kidlington was not assisted by IMSA's summer regulation rethink which restricted two valve stock block engines to 6.0 litres for '88 - that set Engine Division's programme back somewhat.

The GTP car was designed to share as many interchangeable parts as possible with the Group C car for logistical reasons, and again there was a specific Le Mans version of the chassis, though this year it was a more straightforward conversion. Indeed, all three types of car - codenamed XJR-9 - were designed to be interchangeable around a standard monocoque. Three examples were built for each of the two championships with some of these and older tubs converted to form the Le Mans fleet.

A major advantage of this season's two pronged campaign and its multi-purpose car was the potential for an expanded Le Mans operation. Porsche was not going to relinquish its Le Mans rule without a fight and a major strength lay in the depth of its representation. It could push a punishing pace, safe in the knowledge that if all the factory cars broke there would always be private 962C entries to pick up the pieces. TWR anticipated a very hard race - a 24 hour sprint - and planned to bring in its IMSA operation to make up a five car entry. As Doctor Ferdinand Piëch, the architect of Porsche's long standing multi car Le Mans campaign back in the Sixties, remarked to the author: "in a race like Le Mans the number of warships also counted..."

The prototype GTP car emerged in October '87 and had a brief shakedown in England prior to shipment to Daytona for preliminary tests. For the '88 IMSA programme the 6.0 litre high octane engines were built at Kidlington but the cars were run from a new base at Valparaiso, Indiana. The operation was run by ex-Carl Haas manager, Tony Dowe with fellow Englishman Ian Reed in charge of engineering. Reed had engineered March Formula Two cars before moving across the Atlantic with Robin Herd's expansion into the Indy Car market. He had subsequently worked for the crack Shierson Indy Car team. To get to know the TWR Sports-Prototype he and Dowe had run Boesel's winning XJR-8 at Spa Francorchamps in September '87.

Drivers for '88 were Brundle, Cheever, Dumfries and Lammers for Europe and Brundle, Boesel, Watson, Nielsen, Danny Sullivan and Davy Jones for the USA. Sullivan was, of course, an Indy 500 winner while Jones was an American comingman. Playing the key role, TWR favourite Brundle was shunning opportunities with lesser Formula One teams to concentrate upon promoting his career through Sports-Prototype racing.

The 1988 Group C regulations charged the TWR sprint package with running lower diffuser tunnels. Smaller rear wheels were employed which necessitated angling the spring/damper unit.

# Three in One

As we have seen, TWR wanted to keep its various XJR-9 derivatives as close as possible for logistical reasons and in line with this both Group C and GTP cars were equipped with 17" rims front and rear, IMSA regulations demanding equal diameters at both ends. The smaller rear rims made it necessary to angle the coil spring/damper units 10 degrees inwards for clearance, slightly shortening the crossbeam span. However, this was not the handicap it might have been for the Group C car since revised regulations demanded lower diffuser tunnels in '88 (similar in height to those already run on the Le Mans car). Only the GTP car's higher tunnels needed an intrusive blister on the outer wall to make room for the tilt of the spring/damper.

The use of 17" rear rims lowered the rear wheel axis to the normal height of the c.w.p. making it unnecessary to tilt the drivetrain for a reliable 24 hour car. Further, smaller rear wheels required lower arches and the consequent deflation of the bulges in the tail together with a lower set rear wing provided a beneficial reduction in drag, both for sprint and Le Mans versions. That was important for the Group C sprint car given the mandatory lower tunnels. TWR had been exploiting the downforce potential of high tunnels better than anyone and now was forced to look harder at drag.

A drawback of smaller rims was higher tyre revolutions putting more stress on the tyres. Dunlop rig tests suggested that there should not be a problem in terms of vertical loading while the acid test was the Daytona banking with its additional side loading. A Daytona test in late '87 gave the green light to the small wheels.

With 17" rims standard there was little difference between Group C and GTP versions of the XJR-9 aside from weight and tunnel height. All models were based on the same monocoque, essentially that from the XJR-8 but with the seat back/fuel tank bulkhead moved 20mm. forward to allow the GTP car to be fitted with a larger, 120 litre fuel bag behind it. The European and American versions shared the same suspension and transmission (though IMSA's rough circuits called for some heavy duty parts) and either Group C sprint or GTP could be converted to Le Mans specification via a change of clothing. Of course, the GTP model required ballasting to 900kg.

The transaxle had been overhauled for the XJR-9, together with a modification of the rear suspension. The major development was a bespoke TWR main case for the March gearbox, this case offering integral lower wishbone, crossbeam and stay mounts. It also featured sideplates designed to allow the larger c.v. joints run at Le Mans in '87 to be used in conjunction with the regular Salisbury-type TWR/Roni differential.

Detail modifications saw the transmission cooler moved from its upper tail location to the righthand flank, opposite the oil radiator with the lowering of the rear wing, as was standard at Le Mans. A new wiper blade was introduced. At Le Mans in '87 the regular blade had struggled against the Mulsanne airflow and a new, slimmer blade borrowed from the Rover 800 series promised more vigorous action.

Following Percy's Le Mans accident the dependability of Heat Spy operation had been improved, while the tail fixing was revised since after Boesel had failed to secure it properly at Le

Mans it had surprisingly blown open from the back. Consequently, the single central vertical pip pin that had been employed to lock it at the back was replaced by a pair of horizontal pip pins, one on each side. More reliable rear lights were produced in house. These retained only the Land Rover cover - inside were special festoon bulbs while the cover was mounted via TWR's own quick release system.

Clearly, the XJR-9 was essentially a refinement of a proven package. For Group C the 7.0 litre displacement engine went fundamentally unchanged. New for 1988 was a fuel return line running just below the slides within the body of the inlet manifold, this passage offering a chilling effect which saved the weight of a fuel cooler. The only other change was the use of a high quality linear potentiometer to measure throttle angle. This was attached to the slide and was better able to keep up with it. This provided the scope for improved fuelling under transient throttle conditions. With on going development, Scott sought to wring out 750b.h.p. for power circuits.

As we have noted, the IMSA car purposely shared as many components as possible with its Group C sister and this extended to the engine. The key engine differences were those implied by regulations which demanded a maximum of 6.0 litres and offered high octane fuel. With fuel unrestricted Scott sought higher revs from the GTP version. The 6.0 litre displacement consequently came from a combination of the Group C bore and a new short stroke (72mm.) crankshaft. Titanium rods were used but otherwise the internals were those of the Group C engine (including use of a cast iron liner as standard). With detail camshaft work the engine was raced to 7,800r.p.m., pushed harder than the restricted fuel allowance 7.0 litre version.

With the higher quality fuel the compression ratio was taken to 13.5:1 and maximum power with some development became 670b.h.p./ 7,500r.p.m. while torque was 535lb.ft./6,250r.p.m. The engine was still pulling at 8,000r.p.m., the limit to which it was tested on the dyno. Scott reckoned the high quality fuel to have been worth around 25b.h.p. whereas to a turbocharged engine such as the Porsche flat 6 or Nissan V6 it could well have been worth 80/90b.h.p...

Clearly, the GTP car could continue the very effective, high tunnel aerodynamic development programme pursued by Southgate over a period of three years. Southgate notes that throughout there had been subtle nose shape and tunnel development, with "the tunnels always changing". Ducting drag - from brake and radiator intakes in particular - was always under scrutiny while wing endplates were a constant source of change.

Group C regulations for 1988 demanded a larger flat bottom area as well as shallower diffuser tunnels. The mandatory flat bottom area was to be extended to the full width of the car and was to be at least 900mm. long while the diffuser tunnels were to rise to a maximum height of 280mm.

In spite of the extended flat bottom area the tunnels still commenced under the monocoque floor, although they had to be 100mm. shorter. This and the restriction on tunnel height cut downforce at a stroke. However, with intensive work in the rolling road wind tunnel Southgate was able to claw back a good proportion of the loss while improving the lift:drag ratio through subtle reprofiling of the entire underwing and tail (benefiting from the lower rear arches) and careful repositioning of the wing. Outwardly, there was little obvious alteration to the familiar shape of the car aside from the squatter haunches hiding the smaller rear wheels.

The Le Mans version was notable for the return of rear wheel covers. A new method of attachment made the covers easier to replace, since Southgate no longer felt able dispense with them. The experience of '87 had suggested that TWR needed more downforce to go through the Porsche curves more comfortably, particularly in difficult conditions. The Porsche curves represent a significant proportion of a lap at Le Mans and are taken in 3rd/4th gear at around 125m.p.h. Here the XJR-8 had been a handful, low on downforce and somewhat tricky to handle thanks to its tilted drivetrain.

As we have seen, the lower rear arches helped reduce drag and for the LM specification Southgate aimed both to reduce drag and improve downforce. Another 100 runs in the Imperial College tunnel took the total of Le Mans package tests to around 400. According to the 20% models drag was reduced 5% while downforce was increased 13%. The lower arches were helpful, and so was the return of the wheel covers but overall the improvement was due to a great number of mostly very subtle changes.

Apparently, Southgate had looked at a conventional (Porsche Langheck-type) long tail but the XJR-9LM retained the conventional, lower '88 Group C short tail and set the rear wing low in relation to it. Again, in general terms, the wing worked as an extension of the tail - it was an element of the body rather than a conventional rear wing. The wing was set at deck level and the air saw the rear of the car as a long tailed car rather than as a short tailed car with a wing. The wing served to merge the over body and under body airflows, doing so more effectively than a traditional long tail since, as usual, it played an important role in drawing air through the diffuser tunnels.

The 9LM retained the 8LM nose and the same single element wing but the underwing was new. Two chassis - 186 and 287 - were set aside specifically for the Le Mans project, other LMs would be converted from regular Group C and GTP chassis. A new feature of the Le Mans car was electric wing mirrors for adjustment from the cockpit - that was seen as necessary in view of the number of drivers required for a five car assault!

# The German Connection

Although Porsche had pulled its factory team out of the World Sports-Prototype Championship, it vowed to defend its Le Mans throne in 1988. At Weissach the engineers developed new aerodynamics for the one race outing that impressed Southgate, together a more effective engine utilising the sophisticated Motronic MP 1.7 engine management system. As used already by Mercedes, this system governed the wastegate as well as injection and ignition, and offered more precise, more accurate control. It called not only for new (electronically operated) wastegates, but for a complete redesign of the exhaust and turbocharger and intake systems. The turbocharger and aftercooler plumbing was revised, there was just one throttle per bank at the inlet to the plenum, the injectors were repositioned and a new ignition system and new camshafts were introduced. The ignition was now distributorless having three coils, each firing two plugs twice per four stroke cycle and triggered by the ECU.

The more precise engine control upped the detonation threshold, allowing the Typ 935/83 engine to run a 9.5:1 compression ratio. It unleashed more power from a given quantity of fuel and helped put Porsche more on terms with the Jaguar and turbo Mercedes engines that were taking over its pacemaking role in Group C. Nevertheless, aside from Le Mans Porsche left Group C to its customers, as it had done over the latter half of 1987. Some of the key customers had been supplied with conventional Typ 935/83 units following the withdrawal of the works team but not until after Le Mans 1988 would a number of the high compression MP 1.7 versions be made available.

On the World title trail the biggest threat came from Daimler-Benz' decision to grant Sauber's 1988 effort full, open works backing. That meant more cash for the Swiss team, together with technical support and engines prepared not by Heini Mader but in the factory's R&D department. The Daimler-Benz R&D operation was headed by Doctor Panik while Doctor Hiereth was project leader for the development of the Group C engine. The engine designer was engineer Muller while engineer Withalm was in charge of development.

The Group C engine derived from the Mercedes M117 production unit was a 90 degree V8 with bore and stroke of 96.5 x 85mm. for a total displacement of 4970.0cc. which was pressurised by two KKK turbochargers. The M117 had a two plane crankshaft for smooth running at the expense of exhaust tuning potential. However, that was not a serious concern given the forced induction and the smooth, well balanced nature of the unit was considered ideal for an endurance car.

The M117 had an alloy block and alloy, chain driven s.o.h.c. heads. Its two valves per cylinder were offset 20 degrees from the vertical in a wedge-shaped combustion chamber surrounded by generous squish area, which was run in conjunction with a flat topped piston. Although the offset valves were set in parallel they were operated through finger cam followers.

The M117 generally followed the pattern of an earlier iron block M116 V8 engine but offered a massive weight saving in the order of 125kg. thanks to its linerless alloy block. The linerless production block had been made possible through a new production technique, as introduced by General Motors with the famous lightweight Vega 2300 engine. In fact the Reynolds Aluminium developed process and alloy had been pioneered through racing having first been employed as a means of producing blocks for the works Chevrolet-McLaren Can Am car. Reynolds' replacement for the traditional cast iron Chevrolet big block was able to offer increased capacity (8.1 litres) since it was linerless and it was, of course, a lot lighter.

The new generation linerless block was subsequently adopted by both Daimler-Benz and Porsche as a means of producing lightweight V8 engines. The process saw the block diecast by the new 'Accurad' method in a new aluminium alloy, Reynolds A390, which combined good fluidity in the molten condition with a fine dispersion of silicon after heat treatment giving good bearing properties and ease of machining. After machining an electro-chemical etching process was used to expose the glass-hard silicon particles on the walls providing a wear resistant and oil retaining surface.

The production block was run in conjunction with an iron-plated piston skirt to prevent any possibility of aluminium to aluminium contact since that would cause galling (thus the usual combination of alloy piston on iron bore was reversed). However, for the Group C race engine conventional light alloy pistons could be run since the linerless cylinders were Nikasil coated. The race engines were built from production castings which had been taken from the factory and sent to Mahle for a conventional Nikasil coating to be applied to each bore.

The linerless M117 monobloc extended below the crankshaft axis to allow side as well as vertical bolting of the full-width main bearing caps. The four-bolt caps for the five bearings were of cast iron while the race engine's bespoke dry sump (attached via stock studs) was of magnesium and was designed to accept chassis loads. The engine was semi-stressed with loads also fed into the block. The ported alloy heads were attached by six bolts per cylinder and the valve gear was mounted directly on the head. An aluminium rocker cover was retained from the production engine.

The two-plane crankshaft ran in 64mm. diameter plain bearings supplied by Glyco and while lighter than standard was to the same design with the same balancing webs and journal sizes. An in-house production, it was of forged steel and was only polished, receiving no special treatment. As the production crankshaft, the race crank was fitted with a harmonic dampener but this was of a different design in view of the higher revs sought. It was supplied by Goetze. The flywheel was steel, attached by eight bolts and was sized to match a standard 7 1/4 inch clutch with a starter ring around it. The crankshaft was driven by titanium con rods through 48mm. diameter plain Glyco bearings.

The fully machined con rods were of I-section and were supplied by Pankel in Austria. At 170.5mm. eye to eye they were a little longer than standard for a shorter, lighter piston. The Mahle piston was attached by a conventional steel gudgeon pin with circlips and was of the oil gallery type, fed by a single jet. The production head's wedge shaped combustion chamber was retained, the parallel valves inclined to one side with the plug reaching in on the other. The turbocharged race engine differed only in a dish in the piston crown reducing the compression ratio from the stock 10.0:1 to 8.5:1.

The piston carried three cast iron rings, of which the top was chrome plated. The smaller, lighter piston carried smaller than standard rings. American supplier TRW provided the rings at Mahle's recommendation. The special head gasket resembled that of the production car and was supplied by German company Reinz. The head was fitted with Stellite seats for both inlet and exhaust valves which ran in bronze guides. The valves were steel with a Nimonic foot and on the exhaust side were sodium cooled. Dual steel springs were fitted under a titanium retainer.

The production valve gear was retained, with the finger cam followers reducing side loading compared to direct operation of the parallel valves by the cams. However, for the race engine the hydraulic piston atop which the follower's pivot was mounted to provide automatic adjustment was removed, replaced by a mechanically-adjusted stud. The only other modification was a specially hardened plate which was soldered to the top of the steel follower to form the cam working surface.

The camshaft had journals of large enough diameter to allow it to be inserted through bearing holes in aluminium shaft supports, five of which were were bolted to each head. The steel shaft ran directly in its supports and was of a newly devised built-up type produced by a Mahle subsidiary. The method was to produce the cam lobes and the journals separately then to slide them onto the tubular base shaft under a heat process. The resultant shaft was reckoned to be lighter and was less expensive to produce.

The camshafts were driven by a chain off a sprocket at the front of the crank. The double-row chain was a production item and was fitted with a tensioner. Between the front main bearing and the timing drive sprocket was another sprocket, this one to drive the oil pressure pump which was mounted inside the front cover. The scavenge pumps were mounted outside and were driven by a belt from a pulley on the nose of the crank. In fact there were two pulleys, a second belt driving the water pump and alternator.

The water pump was set into the front cover in a central position while the scavenge pumps were to the left of the crankcase, the alternator to the right. Of the five scavenge pumps, three served the engine, two the turbos. Compared to the production engine the dry sump race unit had improved water circulation through enlarged channels - particularly in the head - with twice as much water in circulation.

The alternator was supplied by Bosch, which had developed a distributorless ignition system for the engine. Until mid '87 it ran with a conventional flywheel triggered Bosch CD system. However, with the MP1.7 system, this was replaced by a multi-coil system, the coils triggered by the ECU which took impulses from the flywheel and a camshaft sensor. Rather than having a coil for each plug, one coil jointly served two cylinders and consequently each plug was fired twice per four stroke cycle. This was not, however, found to adversely affect performance. As for the production engine, the firing order was 1-5-4-8-6-3-7-2.

Fuel was injected into the ports rather than the inlet trumpets. The fuel injectors were screwed into the head, as on the production engine, one injector per cylinder. In spite of this arrangement atomisation was considered adequate, "with the valve mostly responsible for atomisation, anyhow", according to engineer Withalm. Earlier the engine had run two injectors per cylinder with the second operating only at full throttle. However, improved injector design and improved control via the switch from MP1.2 to MP1.7 Motronic had allowed one to be dispensed with.

Two throttles were fitted, one just ahead of each entry to the plenum chamber, each turbocharger blowing through its own aftercooler. The inconel turbine turbochargers featured no trickery and had essentially remained unchanged throughout the engine's career. With the MP1.7 system Daimler-Benz produced it own wastegates for electronic control throughout the rev range via the ECU. The driver remained in overall charge of the maximum boost pressure.

The Motronic ECU took readings, apart from those of the crankshaft and camshaft sensors, of charge air pressure as felt in the plenum, air and exhaust gas temperature, water temperature, oil temperature and pressure, fuel temperature and pressure and even turbocharger r.p.m. However, the system retained a plug-in EPROM, unlike the Zytek system now used by TWR. It was used in conjunction with a telemetry system on race day, allowing the engineers to monitor temperatures and pressures. The map provided for the engine in 1988 was based on reference points at 500r.p.m. and 0.1 bar intervals.

By 1988 Daimler-Benz had produced around 30 race engines. Each was reckoned to take two persons one week to strip and rebuild. There were no special qualifying engines but on 2.2 bar absolute manifold pressure qualifying power was quoted as "almost 800b.h.p.". Maximum revs were 7,000 but the driver was asked to observe a limit of 6,500 on race day, aside from overtaking. At the 1.9 bar absolute race setting torque was a massive 800n.m. at 4250r.p.m. and the torque band was spread all the way from 3,000 to 6000r.p.m: sheer grunt was this unit's great strength.

The M117 engine slotted into a well honed chassis that had its roots in the early Eighties. In 1983 Peter Sauber had built a so called C7 chassis to accept a 3.5 litre BMW power plant. He had already built a Cosworth Ford car assisted by three Daimler-Benz R&D engineers working in their spare time, the collaborators including aerodynamicist Rudiger Faul and suspension design expert Leo Ress. Ress had subsequently moved to BMW but retained his Sauber link while Faul was able to get access the fixed floor D-B wind tunnel to evaluate 20% C7 models.

The C7 had a sheet aluminium monocoque and Porsche 956-influenced aerodynamics with a full length central venturi channel recessed into the tub. It was propelled by a BMW engine offering only 450b.h.p. - hence the subsequent switch to the Mader prepared M117, a move made possible by back door D-B support. The M117-C8 that appeared in 1985 was essentially an upgraded C7 design and Ress left BMW to join Sauber as Technical Director in charge of its development.

Ress was able to produce the modified 'C9' chassis for 1987, but this had to retain the existing monocoque. It benefited from new suspension, revised weight distribution and a new approach to aerodynamics, influenced by the XJR-6 rather than the 956. Again 20% models were run in the fixed floor D-B tunnel and the tests involved Ress and 'ideas man' Paul Pfenninninger. Ress reckons he gained 80% more downforce - at the cost of a lot more drag, admitting to a lift:drag ratio 20% worse.

The VGC equipped C9 first tested in March '87, running 100km. at Hockenheim. After two days at Ricard in March it made its race debut at Silverstone in April - and led. Two examples had been built and highlights of a five race World Championship season were the lap record at Le Mans and pole and another lap record at Spa Francorchamps. The model then won the final round of the Supercup at the 'Ring. It was fast but not yet 1000km. (let alone 24 hour) reliable.

During '87 the C9 had gained on its original 880kg. and for '88 Ress looked to less weight, better reliability and less drag for a similar amount of downforce. In spite of the new underwing restrictions he claims to have maintained downforce for 10% less drag. The revised aerodynamics were developed in the usual fixed floor tunnel using the original 20% C9 model modified. Ress reflects that he had, "the benefit of the '87 season - learning how to set up the car for maximum downforce - the influence of car angle: pitch, roll and so forth".

On track, the revised, smaller tunnel underwing would be more critical in respect of pitch, roll and ride height so springs and roll bars would have a much greater influence. In terms of weight, lighter bodywork helped get 001 and 002 - converted from '87 specification to start the campaign - back to 880kg. Later chassis, with detail modifications, would get down to around 865kg. For better reliability there were some uprated suspension parts and, most importantly, major transmission modifications.

Sauber ordered its own c.w.p. from Ate in Finland and gears from Staffs. A new differential was supplied by Xtrak: this was of the Salisbury type but featured "better parts and higher quality fabrication", according to Ress.

Modular BBS wheels were rejected in favour of one piece Speedlines: Sauber didn't get a hoped for weight saving but gained a stronger, stiffer wheel that assisted brake cooling. AP Racing brakes were replaced by Brembo items, Brembo offering a 14" inch disc that saw the front wheels increased from 16" to 17" diameter while the rears remained at 19" diameter. The 14" diameter Brembo discs were 3mm. thicker, featured an original internal ventilation system and were attached by 12mm. rather than 10mm. bolts. They were used with a stiffer, machined from solid caliper that provided more secure attachment to the upright - "the AP caliper always moved in relation to the upright", claims Ress.

The C9/88 retained the traditional aluminium monocoque from the C7, which was produced in house at Sauber's Hinwil, Switzerland base. This ran from firewall to nose box and had a conventional single central-chassis fuel tank. The bulkhead supporting the front suspension was magnesium, the others were aluminium though the rear bulkhead had magnesium sides to receive roll hoop loads. The side boxes were formed by carbon fibre skins over aluminium honeycomb, these panels formed in one piece with an undertray that filled in the redundant 50mm. deep central venturi channel inherited from the C7. The nose box carrying the radiator was also carbon fibre over aluminium honeycomb.

Behind the monocoque, A frames ran back to the bellhousing to leave the engine only semi-stressed. At the front, the engine was attached by sump bolts and a transverse 'torque tube' which ran from the top left of its front cover to the base of the tub on the right hand side. The lateral A-frames were situated within another, more beefy pair of frames that ran directly back from the tub (at right angles to the rear bulkhead) to meet the ends of an extended transaxle yoke. Supported by the main case, this transverse aluminium crossbeam ran between the rear tyres. It supported the front of the upper wishbone while the coil spring/damper units were located on the beefy outer frames, running along the top rail towards the tub.

The unusual rear suspension layout was a response to the high tunnels run in '87 - there was nowhere else to put the dampers, Ress explains. From each upper wishbone, the coil spring/damper unit was operated via a very short link and compact rocker. Advantages of the spring/damper unit location were that the dampers were easily accessible, were easy to cool and were rigidly located - the only serious drawback was in additional time to strip the rear suspension.

Bilstein gas dampers were run at the rear. Sauber had tried Penske Indy Car gas dampers (with remote cylinders to allow pressure alteration) but these would have needed a lot of development to make them survive - the C9 gave its dampers a very heavy time. It ran hard springs and only rarely a rear anti roll bar. Leaving the bar off was good for traction, and more importantly enhanced tyre life.

A second, shorter aluminium crossbeam located the rear of the narrow based upper wishbones while wide based lower wishbones spanned the length of the transaxle which supported them. The wishbones were steel while the rockers working the spring/damper units were aluminium, as were the hubs which ran in welded steel uprights on Timkin taper roller bearings.

Six studs from the outer c.v. joint drove the hub and six pegs formed by the wheel rim took drive from the hub while transmitting it to the disc bell. Ress points out that forming drive pegs with the wheel rather than the hub provided a change of pegs with each change of wheel. The Mercedes V8 was nothing if not harsh upon its transmission. Its torque was so high that gears, c.w.p. and halfshafts had to be changed for each race. The driveshafts came from MAT, a small German company run by an ex-Lobro employee. MAT produced high quality steel shafts, very carefully fabricated and hardened. These were fitted with conventional c.v. joints.

The VGC based transaxle was driven through a conventional 7 1/4 inch AP Racing triple plate clutch housed inside a Sauber bellhousing. The bellhousing was cast in magnesium by Honsel and did not incorporate the oil tank. The tank sat in the lefthand side box alongside the central fuel tank. The side boxes extended back as far as the rear wheels with a turbocharger in the back of each box, close behind the mid mounted aftercoolers. A NACA duct in the top of each box collected cooling air for the turbocharger and its wastegate while a NACA ducts in the side of the box fed the aftercooler and compressor. The turbine and wastegate exhausted through the adjacent side box flank.

The water radiator was located in the nose with its inlet over the splitter, its exit over the screen. Oil was cooled via a heat exchanger, like the water and charge air radiators supplied by Behr and plumbed into the water system. At the rear, over the gearbox was a dual element Sobek radiator for fuel and transmission cooling. This was fed via a NACA duct in the centre of the rear deck. Brake scoops emerged through the deck, feeding down into the top of the rear uprights. Just ahead of the scoops were cooling air intakes for the heavily worked dampers.

The tail was of conventional shape with high arches to accommodate the 19" rear rims and a two element rear wing was outrigged on a single central post. A horizontal plate extending forward under the gearbox endplate supported the rear lower wishbone mount, the air jack and the wing post. The wing overlapped the deck, at the back of which was a low spoiler. The spoiler helped stabilise the car in wet conditions and caused little drag so was a permanent fixture.

Underneath, in broad terms the underwing followed the general form of the XJR-9 underwing from splitter to reduced height tunnel exit, with the entire monocoque floor a flat area. However, the width of the monocoque allowed only narrow horizontal side skirts and there were no rear wheel covers. Two lengths of splitter were available, otherwise the only aerodynamic adjustment was the wing angle. The splitters were rated 'slow' or 'fast' circuit while the wing angle was the crucial tuning device.

For Le Mans '88 the only aerodynamic modification would be a smaller splitter and a single element rear wing, moved back 100mm., to extend the overall length to 4700mm. With its compact V8, the C9 ran on a 2700mm. wheelbase. It had a bellhousing as long as that of the XJR-9 and, as we have seen, a conventional central fuel tank, a mid located oil tank (and battery) and a

The Sauber C9 made its entrance at Silverstone in 1987, where these photographs were taken. Note the unusual location of the rear spring/damper units, keeping them clear of the high diffuser tunnels.

front radiator. Engine weight was quoted as 190kg. including turbocharging system and weight distribution was in the region of 40 - 60.

The front suspension ran Bilstein gas dampers and a steel anti roll bar with three pits-adjustable positions. The C9 had a complex front bar linkage with a push rod from the lower wishbone working a rocker high on the front bulkhead which in turn lifted a pull rod which operated the respective bar arm. This allowed the bar to be low mounted along the front of the monocoque. In contrast, the front suspension was conventional with steel upper and lower wishbones and outboard coil spring/ dampers slung between the front bulkhead and the lower wishbone.

The front uprights were magnesium alloy, cast by Honsel, and again ran aluminium hubs in Timkin taper roller bearings. Once more, the wheel pegs were incorporated in the wheel casting. The 17" front Speedlines were of 13" width whereas the 19" rears were 14.5" wide. The steering was Sauber rack and pinion.

The 14" diameter cast iron Brembo discs were new to Group C having previously been run on Volvo Group A cars. They were of the so called "Pioli" type which set rods between the two plates instead of curved vanes. The distribution of the transverse rods (as evident on a side elevation drawing of the disc) was carefully arranged to have a similar aerodynamic effect to conventional vanes. The staggered rods were a more elegant means of flinging air out of the periphery of the disc: an example of the best in Italian design!

Brembo points to the Pioli disc as lighter and better in terms of the distribution of temperature over the surfaces of the plates. Each disc was claimed to weigh only 6.2kg. It was run with a two piece, differential bore aluminium four pot caliper weighing 3.2kg. Sauber commendably fitted asbestos free pads from the Pagid company in Essen, Germany. At the front cooling was via ducts feeding through the back of the upright. Brembo reckoned the Sauber C9 was the best braking '88 Group C car due to its combination of weight distribution, downforce and effective brake cooling.

The C9 was equipped with an ATL fuel cell housing two pre-pumps ahead of the collector pot, while two high pressure pumps fed the engine. The driver was provided with a fuel consumption read out on the dash, plus warning lights for oil pressure, fuel pressure, oil temperature, water temperature, charge air temperature, exhaust gas temperature, fuel temperature, plenum pressure, and so forth. He also had radio communication with the pits.

Bosch supplied the instrumentation, lights, wiper system and starter motor, Gates the battery. The windscreen was a normal laminated item from a German production car supplier and came via the bodywork manufacturer, which was the local Paucoplast firm. The bodywork employed Kevlar over aluminium honeycomb. The doors had

Plexiglas windows and were front hinged with Renault R5 rear hatch catches!

Aside from its German speaking opposition, in 1988 TWR would face the usual Nissan and Toyota factory opposition at Le Mans and Fuji (Nissan with an improved V8 turbo engine), the enthusiastic Cougar and Peugeot-WM Le Mans teams and, more worrying, the top teams on the Camel GT trail, which were headed by Electramotive Nissan and a number of very professional Porsche outfits.

For 1988 IMSA forced turbo engines as fielded by Nissan and the Porsche teams to run a 57mm. air inlet restrictor. Porsche's IMSA version of the 962 was confined to a 3.0 litre air cooled single turbo engine and Porsche responded to the new air restrictor with an 8.0:1 compression ratio and an engine tuned to offer far more torque if less top end power, under 700b.h.p. Response was faster, power building up very quickly - then the air restrictor cut in, flattening out the power curve.

Porsche did not have the advanced Motronic MP 1.7 engine management available for IMSA hence it GTP teams did not have electronic wastegate control as featured on the Electramotive Nissan. The Electramotive car employed a chassis derived from a mid Eighties Lola GTP machine and heavily modified, the updated version penned by Trevor Harris and built in California by ex-pat Englishman Jim Chapman.

The car was propelled by an Electramotive developed 3.0 litre V6 engine restricted to a single turbocharger and based on a production block and single cam heads. The so called VG30 engine had a four bearing 60 degree vee iron block derived from the production item which was fitted with two valve s.o.h.c. "hemi" heads. The inclined valves were operated by the belt driven centrally located camshaft through rockers, while there was a single plug per cylinder. There was nothing radical about the mechanicals of the engine: the key to its performance was a very sophisticated control of fully electronic injection, CD ignition and the wastegate via Electramotive's own, very powerful engine management system.

*Front end of the Sauber C9/88 revealed. Note the complex anti-roll bar linkage and conventional outboard spring/ damper location. The car ran a traditional sheet alloy monocoque.*

# Third Time Lucky

1988 opened with a major test on the Talladega oval where chicanes were added to simulate the Daytona oval plus road course. Starting the IMSA campaign with the Florida 24 hour race was a daunting task, though happily, as we have seen the XJR-9 was firmly based upon well proven technology. TWR prepared three chassis (running a conventional high speed circuit aerodynamic package, as seen at Monza for example) and Lammers put one of them second on the grid, just 0.4 seconds shy of the 962 pole in single car qualifying. The biggest problem was the conflict between the need for high tyre pressures to run the banking and the loss of traction on the infield section caused by such pressures.

The race pitted the trio of eye openingly fleet newcomers against the massed ranks of Porsches with Holbert Racing the favourite of half a dozen well established 962 teams. As is usually the case, Daytona was a race of attrition and of the top contenders only two teams managed a relatively

*The impact of the 1988 Group C regulations was felt at Paul Ricard where, as usual, TWR sought the winter sun for pre-season testing. Here Brundle watches preparation of a car to XJR-9 sprint specification.*

troublefree run. The XJR-9s surprised the Porsche teams by running strongly from the start and holding their pace for hour after hour after hour... Against expectations, Brundle/Nielsen/Boesel/Lammers ran home victors, just one lap ahead of the top 962. And Cheever/Dumfries/Watson finished 15 laps adrift to claim third place. TWR wore down the opposition, yet lost only one car in the process. A very fine achievement.

Of course, the Daytona result boded well for Le Mans. The '88 Le Mans programme kicked off shortly afterwards at Ricard where chassis 186 ran alongside the new Group C sprint cars and over a period of four days clocked in the region of 15 hours running. After Daytona, the need wasn't felt for a 24 hour endurance test.

All XJR-9 derivatives were now running stronger taper roller front wheel bearings since the regular second generation ball bearings hadn't stood up well to the loading imposed by the Daytona banking. The 9LM ran well on the Ricard long

Further photographs from the Ricard test, illustrating both sprint (left and above) and Le Mans (right) versions of the XJR-9. Both run smaller, 17" rim diameter, rear wheels and thus the common tail is

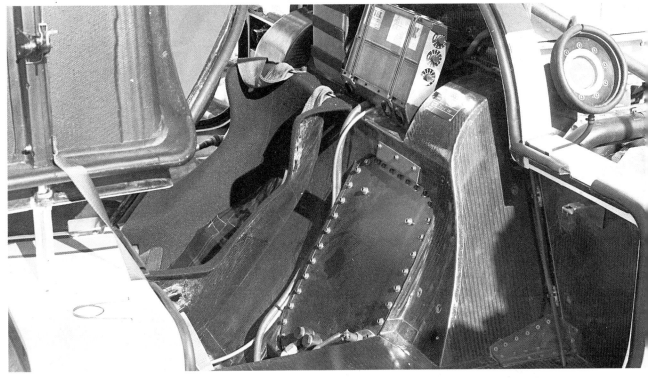

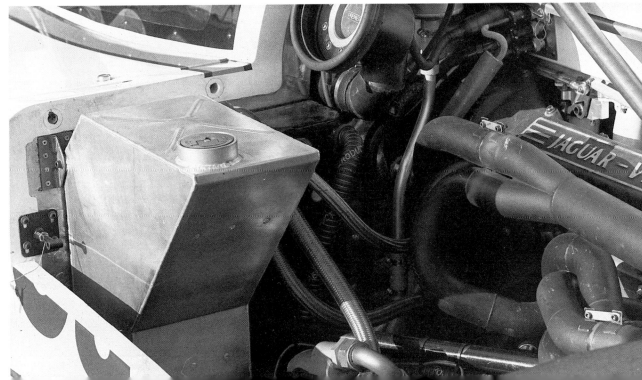

lower. Overleaf the
Le Mans model is
pictured at the
meeting, as is
the rival works
Porsche 962C.

circuit. "We were very impressed by the times", says McQueen, "and could see the extra downforce. The car did as it was told through the corners. And it was a lot nicer to drive with the engine not trying to get over the driver's shoulder. The driver didn't need to concentrate 110% to drive fast".

After Ricard 186 ran all the regular Silverstone tests, though this year there was no Silverstone 1000km. race test. Again, it wasn't seen as necessary given the level of knowledge and experience accumulated. And the ACO couldn't organise a test day since the Mulsanne straight was being resurfaced.

Only slight changes were made to the original 9LM specification as a result of the test programme. For example, the exhaust brackets were made more substantial. Aside from chassis 186, the five race cars prepared for Le Mans included two regular '88 sprint and a regular GTP chassis. All were shaken down at Silverstone well in advance, on the Wednesday prior to Tuesday scrutineering. Watson drove them all to ensure the team would, as far as possible, have five identical cars and he pronounced them almost exactly the same.

Although five cars were to be run, Silman kept the team as compact as possible. The two IMSA crewed cars were run by 21 engineers and mechanics from Valparaiso (travelling direct from the Mid Ohio race) while the other three machines were tended by 41 Kidlington engineers and mechanics. Add to those 62 chassis and engine technicians 14 drivers and 35 others including component support (tyre and brake company representatives, for example), signalling team, timekeepers, the drivers' trainers and so forth and the total army was unavoidably 111 strong.

Of the TWR quintet, the three 'European' cars were headed by #1 - chassis 588, twice a winner in sprint trim - driven by Brundle (it was his regular sprint car) and Nielsen and engineered by Alastair McQueen. Car #2 - chassis 488, with a history of d.n.f. as a sprint car - was driven by its regular pairing of Lammers/Dumfries, assisted here by Andy Wallace. As usual, it was engineered by Eddie Hinckley while car #3 - chassis 287, Boesel's '87 title winning car - was driven by Boesel/Watson/Henri Pescarolo and was engineered by Ken Page.

The two 'American' cars run by the Atlantic crossing IMSA crew were #21 - chassis 188, the regular IMSA spare car that had finished third at Daytona - driven by Sullivan/Jones/Price Cobb and engineered by Ian Reed and #22 - chassis 186 - driven by Daly/Cogan/Larry Perkins and engineered by Dave Benbow. Chassis 186 was making its third visit to La Sarthe and had been recently rebuilt following a Silverstone testing shunt. Chassis 187 was kept in the truck as an emergency spare.

The opposition included three cars - as usual - from the Porsche factory backed by eight private 962C models. The customer line up was still exclusively to Motronic MP1.2 specification and

featured two cars apiece from Joest, Kremer and Brun. Cougar fielded two Porsche-Cougars while the rest of the C1 entry was headed by the two dark blue cars from Switzerland carrying the hopes of Daimler-Benz. Other potential threats included two Nissan V8s, two Nissan V6s and two Toyotas while WM continued its search for 400k.p.h., this year running two low drag specials. Southgate notes that the XJR-9 would have comfortably exceeded 400k.p.h. given the 900 b.h.p. run by WM.

The serious business was going to be a battle between three major manufacturers. Early season World Championship races had shown a far more competitive Sauber with the speed to worry TWR and much improved stamina, though 24 hour endurance was still a question mark over the C9/88. Sadly, though, the Mercedes challenge was thwarted before it could be put to the test.

Early season tests at Monza had witnessed tyre blow outs as a result of which Michelin had developed new construction tyres for the C9 chassis. Those tyres had been tested satisfactorily at Hockenheim then were run without incident in the first Le Mans qualifying session on the Wednesday evening. However, following the resurfacing of the entire length of the Mulsanne straight competitors were invariably finding tyres running hot. Less bumpy, the flat out section of track was providing more download while the new surface was more abrasive. In the second session one of the Saubers blew a tyre just after the kink, thankfully without crashing.

Michelin could give no assurance that the problem would not recur and Sauber withdrew. Mercedes telemetry had shown the rear tyres running hot. However, according to Sauber Technical Director Leo Ress, subsequent tests on a Michelin track equipped with a special pad to measure downforce suggested that the level of download generated by the C9, when multiplied to represent speed around 240m.p.h. was still insufficient to have caused tyre failure.

TWR found its tyres running hot and blistering at first. At a given speed the low drag 9LM had only half as much downforce as the sprint car but on the Mulsanne it was generating as much downforce as the team had ever seen at any circuit in view of the speed and lack of bumps. This year, the car was staying on the track, not bouncing from bump to bump. It was more comfortable to drive and was running its underwing more effectively, though Southgate is suspicious of the higher top speed readings offered by the ACO - up from the 230m.p.h. region to the 240m.p.h. region.

Of course, the impressive Mulsanne downforce was unnecessary, a bye-product of the performance required elsewhere on the circuit. The 9LM demonstrated the sought after gain in grip through the Porsche curves. The Mulsanne tyre blistering problem was solved by going up on tyre pressures. The team initially went up a lot on pressures then gradually dropped back until the problem just started to recur. It then lifted the pressures a little above the danger level and started to sort the chassis.

The lowest safe pressure left the XJR-9LM as an

*Details of the XJR-9LM. Note the pinchbolt securing the lower rear wishbone's rod end in the photograph bottom left, repeated for upper front wishbone as evident above. This sort of thoughtful detail design is the hallmark of a car capable of winning Le Mans.*

oversteering car. That was tackled by the usual chassis and aerodynamic adjustments. By the end of qualifying TWR had a small amount of understeer, which made the '88 Le Mans runner comfortable to drive. In view of the involved setting up process caused by the resurfacing work, only Brundle and Lammers ran qualifying tyres, and then with less than ideal set ups on Wednesday night. Brundle clocked the quickest XJR-9 lap in 3m. 21.78s. while Lammers ran faster - officially 388k.p.h. as against 385k.p.h. - which translates as 241m.p.h.

Brundle bagged fourth on the grid behind the works Porsche trio, pole position won by Stuck with a remarkable 3m. 15.64s. lap - over five seconds under the '87 pole. The works Porsche was officially running the Mulsanne at 391k.p.h. - 243m.p.h. Lammers was sixth quickest, the TWR hot shots split by the fastest Joest Porsche which ran 3m 23.30s. Kremer put one of its cars seventh on the grid, then the remaining three Jaguars were split by the surprising Toyota turbos. Jaguar #3 collided with one of the Toyotas on Wednesday night and subsequently lost its engine: it wound up slowest of the TWR quintet, in twelfth place.

Come Saturday and Stuck's factory Porsche led from the start but by the end of the lap Lammers was up to second and was challenging him. On lap six Jaguar #2 took the lead, and it held off the three Weissach entries all the way to the first round of stops while Brundle gave chase, Jaguar #1 having to be pushed harder to keep the pace. The problems of qualifying had left TWR unsure of the optimum race settings and #1 was running more downforce and without a rear anti roll bar for improved traction. Relatively slow on the straight, Brundle was having to work harder in the corners and that effort wasn't helped by the lack of a rear bar which made the car looser.

Lammers handed to Dumfries after 11 laps while the Porsches ran 13 laps before refuelling. Dumfries came under pressure from Stuck but he was able to keep #2 out in front. Meanwhile the other two works Porsches then the other four Jaguars gave chase, with just three other cars snapping at their heels, the two Joest Porsches and the fastest Brun Porsche. After 70 minutes Jaguar #1 suddenly appeared on the TV monitors stuck in the gravel at Indianapolis. The car's handling had got the better of Nielsen and five minutes were lost as he was towed out.

In the third hour the Stuck/Bell/Ludwig Porsche spluttered out of fuel at Arnage - refusing to pick up its reserve - and Ludwig staggered into the pits on the starter motor, the misadventure costing a couple of laps. Then Lammers had a minor collision, suffering tail damage that took a couple of minutes to repair, then car #22 suffered tyre problems that cost it a couple of laps.

The six hour mark saw the Wollek/Schuppan/van der Merwe works Porsche leading but Lammers/Dumfries/Wallace on the same lap while the Andretti/Andretti/Andretti works

Porsche held station in third place, a lap down and just ahead of Sullivan/Jones/Cobb. In spite of its delay, the third works Porsche was now fifth on that same lap while Brundle/Nielsen and Boesel/Watson/Pescarolo were a lap back, ahead of the two Joest Porsches and the Daly/Cogan/Perkins Jaguar which rounded out the top ten, just three laps from the leader. The Brun challenge had faded but Joest was well poised to profit from attrition among the factory cars...

TWR had told all its drivers to run a comfortable pace and had spent the early hours dialling all the cars into the optimum aerodynamic setting and the right fuel mixture. The cars had been running rich over the first few hours and at the four hour mark had been slightly over the fuel allowance. Now the team was right back on the fuel schedule while Porsche appeared to be looking strong at the expense of fuel consumption.

The #3 Jaguar had never really been in the picture and shortly after midnight became the first major retirement, suffering clutch shaft failure. A faulty heat treatment process had allowed a crack to develop.

Sunday saw the #2 Jaguar claw back into the lead, its position strengthened as Schuppan mistook a pit signal and called at his pit unnecessarily. Then the Andretti car started losing water: a pipe had fractured and this cost four laps. As half distance approached, the #21 car, looking strong in third place suffered worsening vibration which called for a gearbox rebuild. There were problems, too, for the second place Porsche which fell back then retired due to the consequences of a leaking fuel rail. However, the Stuck/Bell/Ludwig car moved back onto the lead lap to keep the pressure on Lammers/Dumfries/Wallace as the race passed the halfway mark.

The 12 hour leader board showed Jaguar #2 and its challenger on 197 laps while Brundle/Nielsen were on 196 laps and the Andretti Porsche was on 194 laps. One and three laps further back were the Joest Porsches, while Jaguar #22 was on 191 laps following minor mishaps and Jaguar #21 was in the pits having its transmission rebuilt.

Daylight brought dazzle for the drivers of the lead car thanks to a cracked screen and this was replaced at the cost of a few minutes delay, enough to put the works Porsche into the lead for the first time on Sunday. However, a precautionary stop to change the water pump pipe on the Stuck/Bell/Ludwig car handed the advantage back to TWR, #2 and #1 running one-two. The Andretti car was no longer a threat - it had burned a piston and was running home on five cylinders. The #21 Jaguar required yet another transmission rebuild as the race approached 18 hours. This time its problem was traced to the clutch spigot bearing not being fitted properly into the flywheel. The first time the transmission had been changed without uncovering the spigot, hence this second rebuild.

At threequarter distance the top six leaderboard was topped by #2 on 296 laps, two laps ahead of the healthy works Porsche and #1 - which had now started overheating - and six laps ahead of the rest, now led by Joest. The #22 Jaguar was sandwiched by the two Joest cars having completed 289 laps. Radiator sealant was tried on the #1 car since it had lost coolant. To no avail: the engine was cooked. At first TWR's first ever head gasket failure was suspected but this was not the case. The culprit was a casting failure. Still - unlike Group 44 - TWR had never lost a head gasket, a tribute to Scott's gasket design, and this was only its second ever (production) head casting failure.

So the race was down to one Jaguar and one Porsche - with one American Jaguar and two private Porsches poised like vultures to pick up the pieces...

The lead car's two lap advantage was cut during an hour of light intermittent rain just prior to midday, Stuck throwing caution to the wind while Lammers was unlucky on tyre choice. And the rain gave Porsche a little help with its overdrawn fuel account. However, though the Porsche was able to unlap itself as Sunday afternoon unfolded, it didn't have the fuel to charge all the way to the flag. Porsche tried to lull TWR into a false sense of security but Silman had the situation well under control and both the Jaguar and the Porsche finished with only a few litres to spare. The Joest team bagged third and fifth places, still sandwiching the #22 Jaguar while the Andretti Porsche ran home to sixth. After its two transmission rebuilds the #21 Jaguar came home in 16th position on 331 laps.

TWR had found it had run too conservatively on fuel in '87 and its '88 winner completed 394 laps - 5332.79km, only three kilometres short of the all time record held by a Porsche 917K since 1971, before the construction of the Porsche curves and the Dunlop chicane. Elsewhere on the World Championship trail, the sprint XJR-9 was often running faster to the fuel thanks to its improved lift:drag ratio. At Monza it was no less than two seconds a lap faster to the fuel. But TWR was finding stronger Group C opposition than ever before in the form of the Mercedes-Sauber C9/88.

Generally speaking, the Jaguar was a better package where fuel was spent overcoming aerodynamic drag, such as at Monza or Silverstone, and by the summer Scott was running 750b.h.p. on 'power' circuits. However, the turbocharged Swiss rival represented a better package where fuel was spent accelerating from low to high speed, such as at Brno or Sandown.

The Sauber was faster everywhere than in '87 thanks to strides in engine and tyre development which followed the increased Daimler-Benz commitment while the XJR-9 had more power yet had lost absolute performance on circuits where downforce counted. Indeed, TWR was hardest hit of all by the reduced tunnel size since it been exploiting tunnels more than anyone else. The smaller tunnels made the XJR-9 more pitch sensitive and Koni dampers appeared on the rear as well as at the front as settings got harder at the back.

Sauber shocked by winning round one at Jerez in convincing fashion then TWR restored its reputation at Jarama, Monza and Silverstone on the run up to Le Mans. However, from Le Mans the circus moved to Brno and here the Mercedes-Sauber showed a clear advantage. The second half of the season saw TWR fighting a defensive game as it strove to retain its World title against an improving, hungry challenger.

The Swiss car was, according to engineer Ress, still hard work to keep running in the transmission department, though with more money parts could be changed more often. The Sauber remained overweight and was hard to set up and difficult to drive quickly. It wasn't a problem for a good driver to handle, though, and it certainly braked and went well. On the right circuit it was more than a match for the XJR-9 thanks to the impressive performance of its turbocharged engine.

Interestingly, Ress reports that a cutdown nose introduced at Brands Hatch improved the performance of the rear wing (at the expense of an insignificant deterioration in cooling) since it improved the airflow over the entire car. Mid season XJR-9 development saw the British car purged of excess kilos - by Brno its weight had risen to around 880kg., matching that of the Sauber. In response the air jacks came off again, and so did any other 'luxury' items, including door seals and other such details. At the Nurburgring a weigh-in with carbon-carbon rather than cast iron discs registered 855kg.

By this stage the XJR-9 had reverted to an oil:water heat exchanger (again positioned under the oil tank). The use of a heat exchanger called for a larger front radiator and in turn a larger front inlet, which added drag. However, the oil radiator in the lefthand flank had bled downforce, so downforce was added.

Brands Hatch saw an exciting new four valve head. This was not a Jaguar Engineering development - it had been designed and produced by Engine Division and the rights to it were owned by Jaguar Sport, a company in which both Jaguar and TWR had a stake. It was a straightforward conversion which, unlike the earlier Jaguar four valve engine, retained the regular front cover. Each bank's usual drive sprocket was lowered a few inches from its familiar position on the outside of the tappet block so as to be suspended from the head. Driven by a shortened chain, this sprocket in turn drove the twin cams via a secondary chain.

While it was known to be of conventional four valve design, details of the new head were not available at the time of writing. It was run with the distributor on the back of an inlet camshaft for improved accessibility. A fatigue crack of the rotor arm caused the prototype four valve engine to fail on its debut in the second car at Brands Hatch. Power at Brands Hatch was quoted as 798b.h.p. and subsequent development appears to have

# CLUB DE L'OUES'

# NS 1988

# HEURES AUTO
# 11 12 JUIN

increased this to 830b.h.p. However, the engine was not seen again. The second car wasn't producing results and a sideways step wasn't perceived as the right move when the team was up against it.

After Le Mans TWR added only Brands Hatch and Fuji while Sauber took Brno, the 'Ring, Spa Francorchamps and Sandown, matching TWR's five sprint/1000km. race wins. It was clear that the XJR-6/8/9 had reached the end of its development potential. It still had a chassis performance advantage but that was no longer a winning edge. An all new car was needed. At the end of the day, however, TWR was again Teams Champion and Brundle was the new World Champion sharing 588 with Cheever. This car retained its original nosebox all season - an unusual occurrence which highlighted the class of its drivers.

Meanwhile, the IMSA programme had been less successful in spite of the efforts of Brundle and his colleagues. After Daytona Miami had seen Nissan quickest but unlucky - the race came down to Jaguar versus Porsche and Jaguar lost by only a fraction of a second. At that stage IMSA looked like shaping up as a close match - only for Nissan to take a firm grip on the sprint races. Nissan shunned Sebring, where Jaguar broke and Porsche won, then took a record eight straight victories. Jaguar was generally best of the rest but did not taste victory again until Del Mar.

*Autosport* remarked: "on the high speed courses where the Jaguars' ground effects wrought excellent cornering, they were out-powered by the Nissan. On the slower courses, the Nissan carried them out of the corners. And on the bumpy street circuits the Jaguars' stiff suspensions and huge anti roll bars kept them off balance... at Del Mar the track's slippery sealant finally gave the Cats and their Dunlops an edge".

Many of the IMSA circuits were uneven, not only the notoriously bumpy street courses and thus the policy of a stiff front end was often severely compromised. In a nutshell: "we had to run softer in the States and that caused more problems", Southgate reflects. In the face of the rough tracks, the GTP car was fitted with strengthened front wishbones and steel rather than titanium springs and the well honed chassis suffered commendably few failures. The steel springs were stronger and less likely to take a set. The American cars also ran Monroe gas dampers, which had remote chambers by which the gas pressure could be adjusted. Effective damping was crucial over the many bumps.

The IMSA campaign was notable for occasional use of new Dunlop radial tyres, which were evaluated but never raced by the Group C team. Radials had been tested on and off since '86 and the '88 Kevlar ply version was still undergoing intense development. It offered better traction, better braking and good turn in for slow corners. However, it didn't behave well when heavily loaded by downforce, leaving the XJR-9 struggling for stability in high speed corners. Radial tyres worked well at the tight Colombus track but were no go at Spa Francorchamps. And for the Group C team, they wouldn't even work at Sandown.

The GTP team experimented with a carbon-carbon clutch, standard equipment in Formula One in '88. However, the wear rate seen in tests was outside the limits TWR found acceptable. A carbon-carbon clutch was not raced on either side of the Atlantic but another first for the GTP team was to race carbon-carbon brakes.

Carbon fibre reinforced carbon (CFRC), or carbon-carbon, discs took over in Formula One in the early to mid Eighties - after a pioneering effort by Brabham in the late Seventies - offering increased braking performance and a significant (unsprung) weight saving, which could be as high as 20kg. The new technology took some while to get established since the material was very difficult to manufacture and operated at a significantly higher temperature than conventional cast iron discs. Internally ventilated versions were developed but a high and narrow working temperature range kept carbon-carbon discs off fully enclosed racing cars in the mid Eighties.

As we have seen, AP Racing had done a deal with the American specialist Hitco for the supply of carbon-carbon. Compared to Carbone Industrie carbon-carbon discs, its discs were more stable, offering a more progressive rise in stopping power with increasing heat while CI discs gave additional bite. It was the 13" diameter ventilated AP Racing discs which were employed by TWR.

For TWR the key advantages of the carbon-carbon brakes were less pedal effort for the driver and instant stopping power. The team found no lap time in the reduction in unsprung weight, though a 15kg. weight saving had to be useful. The main problem was keeping the brake temperature within the narrow working range. Heat dissipation is more difficult with a fully enclosed racing car.

TWR first tried AP's carbon-carbon discs at a mid '87 Silverstone test. Boesel was driving and at first found poor braking performance. He therefore started playing with the brake balance control. Suddenly the brakes hit the critical temperature range and came in with a bang, locking the wheels at the chicane. The car went off. This chassis - 187 - was later shunted for a second time at Silverstone, by non other than Jackie Stewart.

In '88 TWR used carbon-carbon brakes for Group C qualifying from Brands Hatch onwards, though they were never raced as the team preferred to concentrate upon proven technology. However, carbon-carbon brakes were more important for GTP racing. Since Group C was racing to a given fuel allowance heavy braking was to be avoided - the cars tended to glide into the corners. Sprint orientated GTP racing was more cut throat - it was important to be able to dive inside and outbrake other cars. Carbon-carbon brakes were raced for the first time at Sears Point.

Heavy braking on the Camel GT trail showed up a problem that had been just under the surface. The (conventional) disc could float back and forth relative to its bell but could not expand radially without pulling the bell with it. Pulling the bell radially caused it to bell out, putting the disc fractionally out of alignment. IMSA experience showed that it could be put out to a degree that was sufficient to cause pad knock off. In response TWR designed a clever dog drive that allowed a disc to expand without pulling its bell out of shape. Such careful and clever detail development was typical of the TWR Jaguar operation.

The colour photographs on the eight following pages illustrate the XJR-9 on track in 1988. The photographs on pages 153, 160 and 156/157 were taken at Le Mans, while the photographs on pages 154/155 and 158/159 were taken at Monza and Sandown Park, respectively.

The XJR-9 Group C car pictured at Silverstone (here and on the previous double page spread) early in 1988. By the end of the season the XJR-6 derived model was struggling to match the rise of the Mercedes-Sauber. For 1989 there would be a new car: a new era...

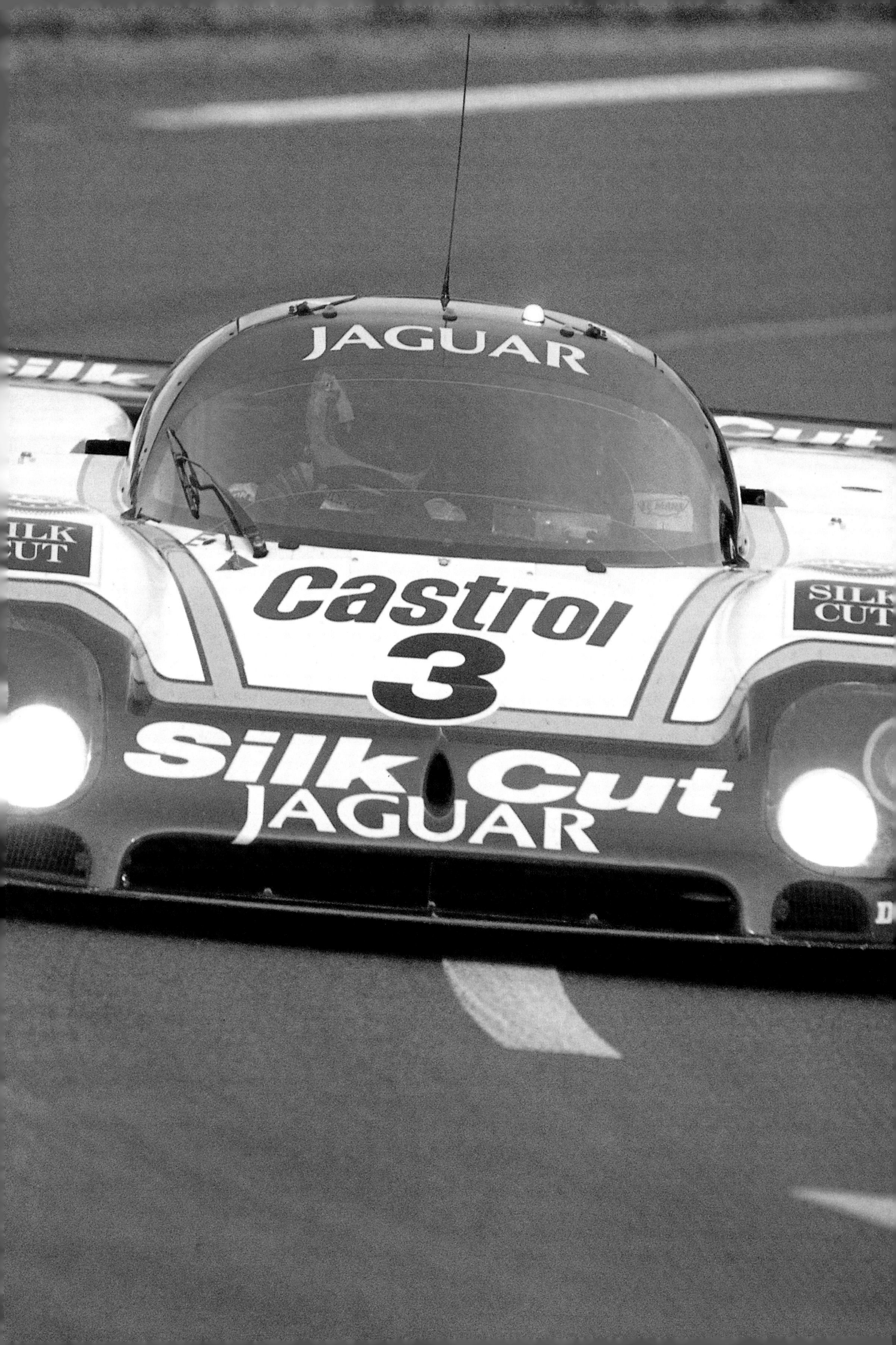
JAGUAR
Castrol
3
Silk Cut
JAGUAR

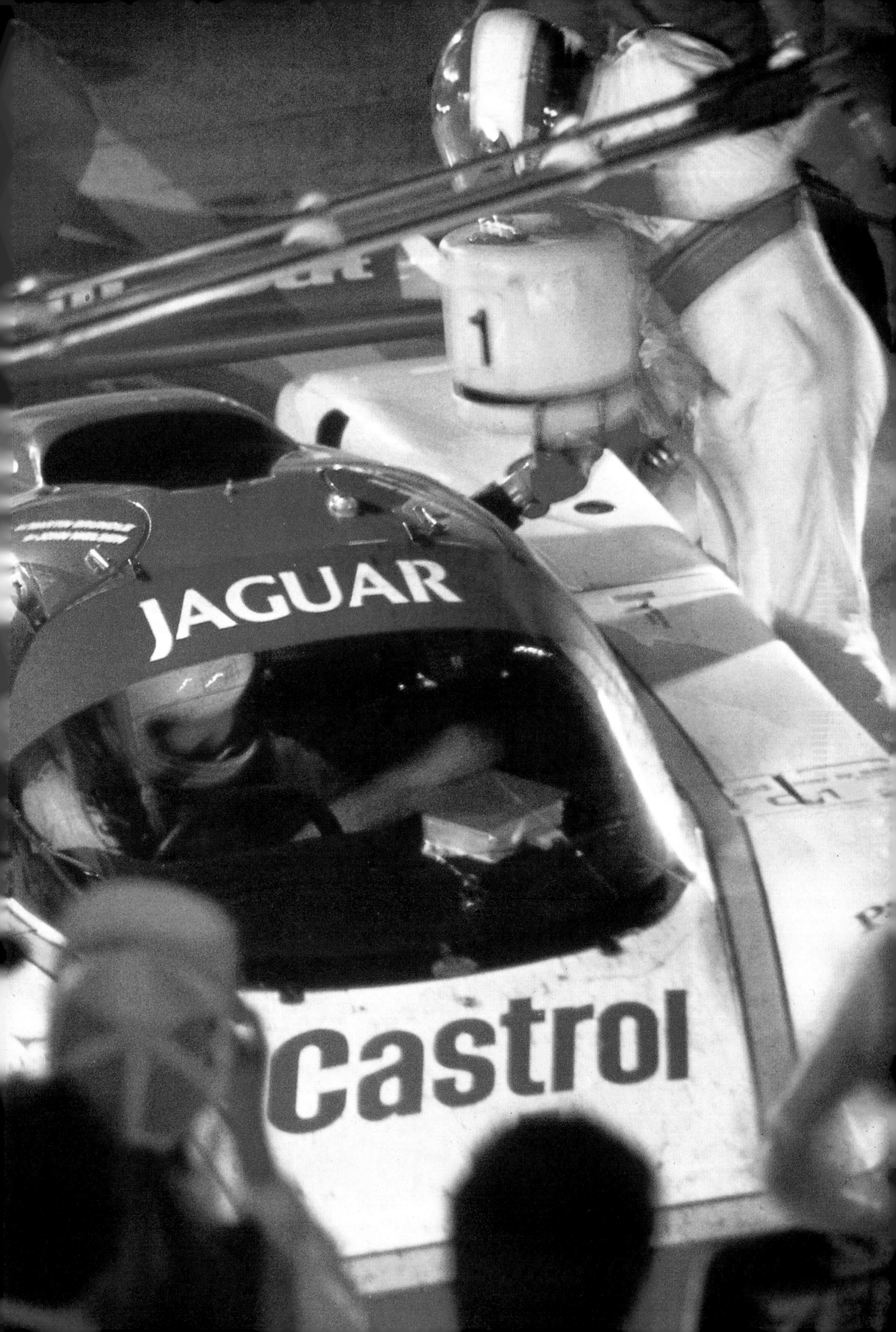

1
JAGUAR
castrol